THE ULTIMATE Toddler Activity Guide

Fun & educational activities to do with your toddler

Written by Autumn McKay

Find me on Instagram!
@BestMomIdeas

The Ultimate Toddler Activity Guide by Autumn McKay
Published by Creative Ideas Publishing

www.BestMomIdeas.com

For permissions contact:
Permissions@BestMomIdeas.com

ISBN: 978-1987787474

Table of Contents

Table of Contents

Table of Contents

Table of Contents

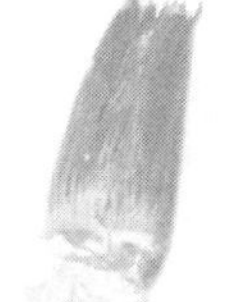

Table of Contents

About Me

My name is Autumn. I am a wife to an incredible husband, and a mother to two precious boys and a sweet little girl! My children are currently 4 years old, 2 years old and 9 months old.

I have a Bachelor of Science degree in Early Childhood Education. I have taught in the classroom and as an online teacher. However, one of my greatest joys is being a mom! After my first son was born in 2013, I wanted to be involved in helping him learn and grow, so I began to develop color lessons to help engage his developing mind. I also wanted to help other moms dealing with hectic schedules and continuous time restraints. As a result, these activities evolved into my first book, called ***Toddler Lesson Plans: Learning Colors***. I continued the daily activities with my son, focusing on learning the alphabet and numbers which turned into ***Toddler Lesson Plans: Learning ABC's***.

Through the last two years I have developed other activities which I have "field tested" with my boys. Both of my boys enjoyed these daily activities so much I decided to write another book sharing all the new activities we have done together. In preparing and developing these activities, I select a theme to focus on and center the activities around that theme. I try to make the activities fun and educational at the same time.

I hope that your little ones can benefit from these activities just like my boys! I have also developed a website called bestmomideas.com to share other toddler activities, as well as tips and tricks of being a mom that I have learned along the way.

Introduction

Nothing is more charming than a child's face and the many expressions of joy a child exhibits in play. Learning can be so fun! Playtime can be an enjoyable moment for the entire family. Throughout these pages you will find many wonderful activities, which hold the potential to bring a smile to your child's face and joy in your home. My hope is that in the midst of your children "playing their way" to growth and knowledge, this book will help flood your home with joy.

As you begin your journey through this book I need to mention that in most of the activities I address your child with the pronoun "he." I did this for simplicity and ease of writing; however, please know, as I wrote this book I was thinking of your precious little girl as well. I also want to reiterate that the goal of this book is to provide you with activities which you can enjoy with your child. The activities in this book are written for the toddler. However, these years are a time of many developmental milestones. Each child is unique, and matures at his or her own pace. If you sense your toddler is becoming frustrated with an activity, please be sensitive and do not push your child to continue. **Without question, you know your child best and what he is capable of attempting.** If you feel an activity is beyond your child's present ability simply move to another activity. There are many great "child tested" activities from which to choose.

Remember, even though significant learning will occur as you engage your child in these activities, I want you and your child to have fun! Often when my preschooler prays, he ends his prayer with the statement, "...And let us have a fun day, Amen." In the midst of hectic days and the constant pressure to perform, a child deserves a fun day. The truth is you deserve a "fun day" as well. It is my desire that in the following pages you will discover a path for your toddler to learn, and an avenue through which you will experience immense satisfaction as YOU have a fun day and enjoy your child.

Additional Helpful Hints

This book includes activities from many different topics toddlers are naturally curious about such as space, parts of the body, senses, the ocean and many more. I recommend reading through the table of contents to find a theme that interests your toddler. Once you find a theme your toddler will enjoy, you can turn to the corresponding page to find a materials list and step by step instructions for each activity. Each activity should only take 10 to 15 minutes because we all know that a toddler's attention span is very short.

For each activity, I suggest you ask your toddler if he wants to do a fun activity instead of making him do it, so that the learning experience is enjoyable. Some days, my boys will tell me they do not want to do an activity, and that is totally fine! However, most days both of my sons will ask me if we can do an activity after I lay their little sister down for a nap. It makes this mommy's heart happy knowing they want to learn!

I recommend doing the holiday themed activities with your toddler during each holiday, or the week leading up to the holiday. This will help your toddler understand that holidays come at different times of the year. It is also a special way to celebrate each holiday.

I know many parents are very busy and don't have a lot of time to set up an activity, so I have placed a "low prep" ribbon beside all activities that should only take a minute or two to prep. I hope these low/no prep activities make life a little easier for you, especially on busy days.

I try to keep an assortment of school supply items in my house to be used for activities so I do not constantly have to run to the store. Here is a list of materials used consistently for many of the activities throughout this book if you want to stock up:

- construction paper
- glue (sticks work best for toddlers)
- crayons
- scissors (adult and toddler)
- paper plates
- beads
- washable paint
- paintbrushes
- painter's tape
- index cards
- markers
- mason jars
- assortment of stickers
- food coloring
- pipe cleaners

We also love to use Do-a-Dot markers, but these are not necessary to buy. To help you prepare your materials in advance, I suggest looking ahead at the next theme you want to do with your toddler and making a list of all the materials you will need to buy during your next grocery shopping trip.

I hope these activities bring as much joy and learning to your home as they have mine!

A Gift For You

On appreciation of your purchase of this book, I would like to provide you with a link to the printable appendix pages. This will allow you to have access to appendix pages in color and do your toddler's favorite activity again and again.

www.bestmomideas.com/sendmyultimateprintouts

Password: bestmomideas6p75

Activities

Body Part Activities

LOW PREP Sticker Labeling

Materials:

- ☐ Stickers

Directions:

Ask your toddler if he would like to play a fun game in which he puts a sticker on the body part you call out. Explain to him that when you say a body part, like ears, he needs to find that body part. After he finds the body part, hand him a sticker to place on the body part.

You can also play the game by calling out a body part and allowing your child to put the sticker on you. My children thought it was quite funny to see me covered in stickers.

Body Puzzle

Materials:

- ☐ Body Puzzle Activity Page (Appendix A)
- ☐ Scissors
- ☐ Construction Paper
- ☐ Glue
- ☐ Crayons (optional)

Directions:

Ask your toddler if he would like to put together a puzzle. Show him the *Body Puzzle* activity page and tell him he is going to put the body back together. You can cut out the pieces, or if your little one has used scissors before, you can let him help you cut out some pieces. Let your toddler put all the body parts together without glue. Ask him where the belly is; when he finds it ask him to lay it in the center of the construction paper. Now ask him to find two arms. Ask him where the arms go. Continue to do this with each body part. Once the person is together, he can glue all the pieces to the construction paper and color it.

Move Your Body Game

Materials:

- ☐ Move Your Body Activity Page (Appendix B)
- ☐ Scissors
- ☐ Glue or Tape

Directions:

You will need to construct the dice from the *Move Your Body* activity page. You can cut out the outline of the two dice, and then fold along the dotted lines. You will then tuck the gray flaps under each white square and either glue, or tape them in place.

Ask your toddler if he would like to play a silly game. Tell him he will roll the two dice, and then you will read the top square to see what it tells both of you to do. Show him an example. If you roll the dice and one says bend and the other says elbow, you will both bend your elbows. Have fun playing with your little one.

LOW PREP How Many?

Materials:

- ☐ How Many? Activity Page (Appendix C)
- ☐ Crayons

Directions:

Ask your little one if he would like to count his body parts. Show him the *How Many* activity page. As you read each sentence to your toddler, point to each word. This will help him understand that you read left to right. After you read the sentence, ask him to count how many of that body part he has on his body. For example, if you read "I have __ eyes," ask him to find his eyes and count them. After he counts them, ask your toddler to find the number two at the bottom of the page so he can see how to draw the number two in the blank. It's ok if you need to draw dotted lines for him to trace.

LOW PREP Body Part Bubble Pop

Materials:

- ☐ Bubbles

Directions:

Ask your toddler if he wants to pop bubbles using his body. When you blow the bubbles, call out the body part your toddler should use to pop the bubbles. You can call out head, toes, fingers, knee, elbow, nose, belly, etc.

Community Helper Activities

Dentist

LOW PREP

Paint a Tooth with a Toothbrush

Materials:

- ☐ Tooth Activity Page (Appendix D)
- ☐ Toothbrush
- ☐ White Paint
- ☐ Paper Plate

Directions:

Ask your toddler if he would like to paint a picture of a tooth using a toothbrush. You can trace the tooth from the activity page onto a colored piece of paper, but you don't have to. Squirt some white paint onto a paper plate. Tell your little one that he is going to use the toothbrush to dip in the paint and paint the tooth.

Explain that he needs to brush the whole tooth because we clean our teeth by brushing all of them. You can also tell your little one that we go to the dentist's office so the dentist can check our teeth and make sure we are doing a good job brushing.

Floss

Materials:

- ☐ Four Prong Mega Block Legos
- ☐ Playdough
- ☐ Yarn

Directions:

Break off three small pieces of playdough and stick the playdough in between the prongs of the mega block. Show your toddler that the mega block is like teeth in our mouth, and when we eat food sometimes pieces of the food get stuck in between our teeth. Tell him that the pieces of playdough are like little pieces of food stuck in between our teeth.

Now he will use floss to remove the food, to keep the teeth clean. Show him how to use the yarn as floss. Show him how to take the piece of yarn and pull it tight using both hands. Slide the tightened yarn under the playdough and lift the playdough away from the mega block. This is something he will probably enjoy doing many times!

Smile Snack

Materials:

- ☐ Apple Slices
- ☐ Peanut Butter
- ☐ Mini Marshmallows
- ☐ Plate
- ☐ Knife

Directions:

Ask your toddler if he would like to make a smile snack. First, you will need to slice an apple. We used red apples so they would look like lips. Place one apple slice flat on a plate and ask your toddler to spread a little peanut butter on the white part of the apple. Now ask him to place mini marshmallows along the edge of the apple peel in the peanut butter. The mini marshmallows should look like teeth. Ask your toddler to spread peanut butter on the white part of another apple slice. Now your little one can place the apple slice on top of the mini marshmallows, peanut butter side down. Enjoy your smile snack!

Doctor

LOW PREP Doctor Tool Sorting

Materials:

- ☐ Doctor Tools Activity Page (Appendix E)
- ☐ Scissors
- ☐ Glue

Directions:

Ask your toddler if he would like to learn about the tools doctors use. Show him the *Doctor Tools* activity page. You will need to cut out the pictures from the bottom of the page. Your toddler is welcome to cut out the pictures, if your toddler wants to try. After the pictures are cut out, show your toddler there is a "yes box" where he will put the tools doctors use, and there is a "no box" where he will put tools doctors do not use. Hold up a picture, ask him what it is, and then ask him if a doctor uses it. Let him place it in the correct box and glue it down.

For example, hold up a picture of a stethoscope, and ask him what it is. You might have to help him with the name. Now ask him if he has seen this tool when he goes to the doctor. He should say yes. Let him glue the stethoscope picture in the yes box.

Band Aid Letter Cover Up

Materials:

- ☐ Box of Band Aids
- ☐ Marker
- ☐ Half a Piece of Poster Board

Directions:

You will need to do a little prep before starting this activity. Cut a piece of poster board in half (You will use the other half during the farm activities). Draw a human outline onto the poster board. Mine was more like a gingerbread man shape. Make sure you try to fill the whole poster board. Now write ABCs (all uppercase letters) all over the person, in random order.

Ask your toddler if he would like to play a game where he pretends to be a doctor who puts band aids on letter boo-boos. Tell him you will say a letter, and he has to find the letter on the person, in order to put a band aid on the letter. It is helpful to call the letters out in order since they are already mixed up.

LOW PREP Glitter Germs

Materials:

- ☐ Hand Sanitizer
- ☐ Glitter

Directions:

Ask your little one if he would like to see how germs are spread. Squirt some hand sanitizer in his hands, and then pour some glitter on top of the hand sanitizer. Ask him to rub his hands together until glitter is all over them. Now ask your toddler to go around the room and shake hands with you, touch toys, the light switch, open the door, read a book, etc. After he has had enough fun touching things, ask him to look at his hands to see if all the glitter is still there. Now have him look around the room for glitter. He should find spots where glitter transferred from his hands.

Tell your little one that germs are like the glitter on his hands except we can't see germs. Every time we touch something or someone, we spread germs. Some germs can make us really sick. This is why we need to wash our hands. Now have your toddler wash his hands with soap and water to see what happens to the germs. Most of the glitter germs should wash away.

Fireman

Community Helper Activities

LOW PREP

Fire Safety Experiment

Materials:

- ☐ Two Candles
- ☐ Matches
- ☐ Large Jar
- ☐ Small Jar

Directions:

Ask your toddler if he would enjoy an experiment with fire. Tell him you are testing to discover how long a covered flame will continue to burn. Show him two candles. Tell him you will light the candles. After you light the candles remind your toddler that candles can become very hot and should not be touched! Now tell your toddler that oxygen helps fires burn. Explain that oxygen is the air you breathe, and it's all around us.

Now show your toddler the two jars. Show him the jars are two different sizes. Tell your toddler you are going to put the jars over the candles to see which candle stops burning first. Carefully place the jars over the candles. Ask your toddler which candle he thinks will go out first. After the flames go out, explain that the fire went out because it used up all of the oxygen in the jar. Explain to your toddler that the smaller jar had less oxygen. So, the candle in the smaller jar went out first.

Squirt the Fire

Materials:

- ☐ Squirt Bottle
- ☐ Water
- ☐ Scissors
- ☐ Crayon
- ☐ Red, Yellow, and Orange Construction Paper

Directions:

Cut out numerous fire flames of various sizes from construction paper. (I cut out 25 flames because I was working on numbers 1-10 with my 2 year old and numbers 1-15 with my 4 year old.) After you cut out the flames, use your crayon to write one number on each flame. Spread the flames out in the bath tub.

You may choose to write ABCs on the flames instead of numbers. You may choose to write the letters from your toddler's name on the flames. If your toddler is still working on color recognition you could cut out one flame from each color. It is totally up to you.

Ask your toddler if he is ready to be a fireman and squirt out the fire. Show him all the flames in the bathtub. Give him the squirt bottle filled with water and tell him it is the fire hose he will use to squirt the fire. Explain that you will call out a number and he will need to find the number and squirt it to put out the fire. My boys loved being firemen!

LOW PREP Crawl Under the Smoke

Materials:

- ☐ Sheet

Directions:

Ask your toddler if he would like to practice crawling under smoke from a fire. Place a sheet over a few chairs or a table. Explain to your toddler that fire makes a lot of smoke and smoke makes it really hard to see and breathe. If there is ever a fire at your house, you want him to be able to get out of the house safely. Explain that smoke rises, so he will need to get really low to the ground and crawl on his hands and knees or even slither on the ground like a snake. Tell him to pretend the sheet is smoke, and that he needs to crawl under the smoke to get outside safely. You can show him how to crawl.

Mailman

Deliver Mail

Materials:

- ☐ Construction Paper
- ☐ Tape
- ☐ Crayons
- ☐ Bag

Directions:

Ask your little one if he would like to play mailman where he picks up letters and delivers them to people's mailboxes. Tell him that first, he will have to make some mailboxes. (Each member of our family made one.) Let each person pick a colored piece of construction paper and fold it almost in half—you will want to leave a little lip at the top to make it easier for the mailman to slide letters into the mailbox—then tape up the sides. Write each family member's name on the mailbox so the mailman can clearly see who to give the correct letter. Decorate the mailboxes. Next, place the mailboxes on the appropriate family member's bedroom door, on a wall, or on the refrigerator.

Now it's time to write letters. Let each member of the family write a letter to another family member. Encourage each family member to write a sweet note or draw a picture. Make sure the name of the person the letter is for is clearly written at the top of the letter, so the mailman will be able to match the names with the correct mailbox. After the letters are written ask the mailman, your toddler, to come pick up all the mail.

He can use a bag in which to place all of the mail. After he picks up the mail, ask him to pull out a letter. You might have to help him read the name on it. Next, ask him to place the letter in that person's mailbox. See if he can match the name on the letter to the name on the mailbox before you show him where the correct mailbox is located. Once all the mail is delivered, each family member can open his or her mail. This is a fun game that we played all week.

LOW PREP Mail Counting

Materials:

- ☐ 10 Envelopes
- ☐ Marker
- ☐ Counters (Post-it notes, pieces of paper, coins, etc.)

Directions:

Ask your toddler if he would like to count mail. Write numbers 1-10 on the flap of each envelope—each envelope should have one number. Lay the envelopes in numerical order in front of your toddler. Count the numbers together. Now explain to your toddler he is going to place the same number pieces of mail in the envelope, as the number written on the envelope. You can show him an example.

For example, show him the envelope with the number four on it. Now count out four objects (counters: representing four pieces of mail) and place them inside the envelope.

LOW PREP Mail a Letter

Materials:

- ☐ Paper
- ☐ Crayons, Pencil, Markers
- ☐ Envelope
- ☐ Pen
- ☐ Stamp

Directions:

Ask your toddler if he would enjoy mailing a letter to someone. It could be a grandparent, aunt, uncle, friend, etc. Encourage him to draw a picture or write a sweet note on the letter. Help him fold the letter to fit in the envelope. Let your toddler slide the letter inside the envelope. Let him lick the envelope and seal it. Show him how to place the stamp on the top right hand corner of the envelope. You will probably need to write the return address and recipient's address since it needs to be small. Walk to the mailbox with your little one and allow him to place the letter in the mailbox and raise the flag. He will probably want to watch for the mailman to come pick up his letter.

Police

Paper Plate Police Car

Materials:

- ☐ Paper Plates
- ☐ Blue Paint
- ☐ Paintbrush
- ☐ Black, Red, and White Construction Paper
- ☐ Glue
- ☐ Scissors

Directions:

Ask your toddler if he would like to make a police car. You will need to cut a paper plate in half. Now lay the paper plate half in front of you with the straight edge facing you. You will want to make an L-shaped cut at the 2 o'clock position of the paper plate. Make a backwards L-shaped cut at the 10 o'clock position of the paper plate. Remove those L-shaped cuts from the paper plate. The plate should look similar to a car shape now.

Let your toddler paint the car blue while you cut out two black circles from construction paper for the wheels. Cut out a white rectangle for the window. Cut out a red rectangle to be the siren at the top of the police car.

Once the paint is dry, let your toddler glue the white window onto the police car. Place the window in the top portion of the car. Let him glue the wheels to the bottom of the police car. Now let him glue the siren to the top of the police car. You can help him write the word "police" in the center of the police car to finish it.

LOW PREP Build a Police Officer

Materials:

- ☐ Police Officer Activity Page (Appendix F)
- ☐ Crayons or Paint
- ☐ Scissors
- ☐ Glue

Directions:

Ask your toddler if he would like to make a police officer. Tell your little one that police officers protect us and keep us safe. Police officers help people who need help. Show him the *Police Officer* activity page. You can let your little one color or paint the police officer pieces first. Next, cut out the pieces and let your toddler put the police officer together. Once he has the pieces in the correct place, let him glue the pieces together.

LOW PREP 911 Collage

Materials:

- ☐ 911 Activity Page (Appendix G)
- ☐ Blue Tissue Paper or Construction Paper
- ☐ Glue

Directions:

Tell your toddler that if he ever needs help from a policeman or fireman, he can call 911. You may want to show him how to dial 911 on your phone. Show him the *911* activity page. Tell him that he can tear the blue paper into little pieces. After he tears the paper, let him spread glue all over the "9," and then he can place the blue pieces of paper on the "9." Do the same thing for the "1s". When your toddler finishes, ask him who he should call if he needs help. Ask him what number he should dial.

Emotion Activities

Feelings Faces

Materials:

- ☐ 7 Craft Sticks
- ☐ Scissors
- ☐ Tape
- ☐ Marker
- ☐ Pink, Red, Orange, Purple, Green, Blue, and Yellow Construction Paper

Directions:

Cut out a big circle from each color of construction paper. Use your marker to draw a happy face on the yellow circle. Draw a sad face on the blue circle. Draw a sick face on the green circle. Draw a mad face on the red circle. Draw a sleepy face on the orange circle. Draw a scared face on the pink circle. Draw a surprised face on the purple circle. Now tape a craft stick to the back of each face—underneath the mouth.

Show the feelings faces to your toddler and talk about each feeling. Think of a story for each feeling to share with your toddler and let him hold up the feeling face that matches the story. For example, I feel ___ when someone takes my toy. In response, your child would probably hold up the mad or sad face.

You can put the feelings faces in a jar and explain to your toddler that he is welcome to pick out a feelings face anytime he has a feeling he needs to talk about.

Emotion Sorting

Materials:

- ☐ Magazine
- ☐ Scissors
- ☐ 2 Paper Plates
- ☐ Marker

Directions:

Go through a magazine and cut out pictures that are happy and sad. These can be pictures of happy or sad people or situations and events that make your toddler happy or sad. Now write happy on one paper plate, and draw a smiley face. Write sad on the other paper plate, and draw a sad face.

Ask your toddler if he would like to play a game. Tell him that you will hand him a picture, and he will decide if it's something that makes him happy or something that makes him sad. Tell him that if it makes him happy then he will put the picture on the happy plate with the happy face, but if the picture makes him sad, he will put the picture on the sad plate with the sad face.

LOW PREP Make Faces

Materials:

- ☐ Mirror

Directions:

Ask your toddler if he would enjoy making faces in the mirror. Let him sit in front of the mirror. I had my sons sit on the bathroom counter in front of our mirror. Tell him you will say a feeling and he should make a face to match the feeling. You can show him the *feeling face* if he needs help knowing what face to make, or you can make the face in the mirror. It is fun to watch him try to make the different faces!

LOW PREP Feelings Line Tracing

Materials:

- ☐ Feelings Tracing Activity Page (Appendix H)
- ☐ Crayons

Directions:

Ask your toddler if he would like to work on tracing some silly lines. Tracing these lines will help him develop his prewriting skills, skills needed to write letters and words. Show him the *Feelings Tracing* activity page. Explain that he will trace the line from the face to the word. Let him try tracing the line with his finger. Now let your toddler pick out a crayon to trace the lines. Do this for each line.

LOW PREP Feelings Chart

Materials:

- ☐ Feelings Chart Activity Page (Appendix I)
- ☐ Crayons
- ☐ Jar
- ☐ Feelings Faces

Directions:

This activity is really an all day activity to help your toddler understand his feelings might change throughout the day. When your toddler wakes up in the morning ask him how he is feeling. Ask him to pick the "feelings face" from the jar that matches the way he feels and place it in the jar beside the *Feelings Chart* activity page. Now ask your toddler to draw that feeling face in the box next to morning on the feelings chart. Do this in the afternoon and evening as well. As your toddler attempts to identify his feelings throughout the day, it will help him recognize his feelings are not always the same.

Farm Activities

LOW PREP Herding Sheep

Materials:

- ☐ Cotton Balls
- ☐ Tongs
- ☐ Ice Cube Tray, Bowl or Cup

Directions:

Ask your toddler if he would like to be a sheep farmer today. Throw a bunch of cotton balls all over the floor. Explain to him that someone left the gate open and the sheep escaped. He needs to herd them back in to their fenced in area so they will be safe. Tell your toddler the fence is the ice cube tray, bowl, or cup, and he will use the tongs to pick the sheep up and take them back to their home. My oldest son wanted me to time how fast he could herd his sheep.

LOW PREP Corn Kernel Sensory Bucket

Materials:

- ☐ Bag of Corn Kernels
- ☐ Big Bowl
- ☐ Spoons, Scoops, Bowls, Measuring Cups

Directions:

Explain to your little one that farmers grow corn on their farm, and that the corn kernels are dried up pieces of corn. Ask him if he would like to play in the corn kernels. Dump the bag of kernels in a big bowl and show your toddler the spoons, measuring cups, and bowls he can use to scoop, pour, and transfer the corn kernels. This activity was a favorite for my sons! We played this almost 30 minutes every day for a week.

Life Cycle of a Chicken

Materials:

- ☐ White, Brown, and Yellow Construction Paper
- ☐ Scissors
- ☐ Crayons
- ☐ Glue

Directions:

You will need to cut a big circle from the white construction paper—this will be where you place each life stage of a chicken. Cut out two small eggs from the white construction paper. Cut out some small strips of brown paper for the chicken's nest. Cut out a medium oval from the yellow construction paper.

Ask your toddler if he would like to learn how chickens grow up. Place the large white circle in front of him. Explain that chickens start out in an egg. Show him the small, white egg that you cut out. Explain that the egg stays warm in a nest. Tell him that he can rub some glue on the top of the big circle, and then place the strips of brown paper on the glue to make a nest for the egg. Next, he can glue the egg in the nest. Now help your toddler draw an arrow to the 3 o'clock position of the big white circle.

Show your toddler the other small egg you cut out and explain that as the baby chicken matures in the egg, the chicken will grow stronger and larger. Tell your toddler that eventually the chicken will need to crack open the egg so he can come out. Let him draw some cracks on the egg, and then he can glue it under the arrow. Help your toddler draw another arrow to the 6 o'clock position of the big circle.

Show your toddler the yellow oval and explain that when the baby chicken comes out of its egg it is a chick. Let him glue the yellow oval to the left of the arrow. Next, let him draw two wings on the sides of the oval, two eyes, a beak, and two feet. Help your toddler draw an arrow to the 9 o'clock position of the big circle. Explain that the chick eats a lot of food and grows up to be a big chicken. Instruct your toddler to place his hand above the arrow, allowing you to trace his hand. Let your toddler color in his hand and add a wing, eye, beak, and two feet. Help him draw an arrow back to the egg in the nest. Tell your little one, it is the big chicken, which lays an egg. Ask your toddler if he can tell you the stages of a chicken's life.

Milk a Cow

Materials:

- ☐ Half a Piece of Poster Board
- ☐ Marker
- ☐ Crayons
- ☐ Surgical Glove
- ☐ Rubber Band
- ☐ Water
- ☐ Pin
- ☐ Tape
- ☐ String
- ☐ Bowl

Directions:

You will need to do a little prep work before this activity. If you did the *Band Aid Letter Cover Up* activity, you should still have half a piece of poster board. Draw a cow on that piece of poster board, color it, and cut it out. It's ok if you aren't an artist, your toddler will still enjoy the activity! I taped the cow to a kitchen chair. Fill the surgical glove about 2/3 full of water and tie a rubber band around the top. Use some string to tie around the top of the surgical glove and tie the other end of the string to the chair so that the glove will hang down where udders are on a cow. Place a bowl under the udders, and then use a safety pin to poke a hole in each udder.

Now ask your toddler if he wants to pretend to be a farmer and milk a cow. Show him that farmers have to milk cows by pulling down on the udders to get milk for us to drink. Let him try. It was difficult for my sons at first, so I ended up poking a bigger hole in the udders for them.

LOW PREP Make Butter

Materials:

- ☐ Mason Jar
- ☐ Heavy Whipping Cream
- ☐ Honey (optional)

Directions:

Ask your toddler if he would like to make butter. Explain to your toddler that farmers use the milk from cows to make butter. Let your toddler help you pour room temperature heavy whipping cream into the mason jar. Fill it about half full. You can add a squirt of honey if you'd like to make honey butter. Screw the top on tightly. Let your toddler shake the jar as hard as he can until the cream starts to turn to butter. Enjoy the homemade butter on a piece of toast!

LOW PREP Farm Animal Sorting

Materials:

- ☐ Farm Animal Sorting Activity Page (Appendix J)
- ☐ Scissors
- ☐ Glue
- ☐ Crayons

Directions:

Ask your toddler if he would like to count the legs of different farm animals. Show him *the Farm Animal Sorting* activity page. Let him color the animals if he would like. Next you can cut out the animals from the bottom of the page. If your toddler has used scissors before you can let him try cutting out the pictures. Show your toddler the two columns and tell him that one box is for animals with two legs and the other box is for animals with four legs. Show your toddler one of the animals and let him count the legs on the animal—you can help count if he needs assistance. Ask him how many legs are on the animal, and ask him to glue it in the correct box. Do this for each animal.

Find the Pig Tails

Materials:

- ☐ Brown Rice
- ☐ Bucket or Pan
- ☐ Multiple Colored Pipe Cleaners
- ☐ Construction Paper
- ☐ Scissors
- ☐ Tongs (optional)

Directions:

You will need to do a little prep work for this activity. Make sure you have the same color of construction paper as you do pipe cleaners. I used the colors yellow, blue, green, red, black, pink, orange, and white. Cut your pipe cleaners into four inch pieces. Curl a pipe cleaner of each color around your finger to make it look like a pig tail. Now you will want to cut out "pig bottoms" from construction paper to match your pig tails. I drew a circle pig bottom on top of two rectangle pig legs and then cut them out. Pour your brown rice in a bucket or pan and mix your pig tails into the rice. Lay your pig bottoms in a line close to the rice bucket.

Tell your toddler that something silly happened. All the pigs were rolling around in the mud and lost their tails. Ask him if he can help you find the right pig tails to match each pig. He can use tongs or his hands to search for the pig tails. When he finds a pig tail, ask him to match it to the correct color pig bottom.

Fine Motor Activities

LOW PREP *Peel Tape*

Materials:

- ☐ Painter's Tape

Directions:

Place various lengths of painter's tape on your kitchen table, hardwood floors, or cabinet. The pieces of tape can cross or overlap.

Ask your toddler if he can help peel the tape off. You might need to show him how to start. Praise him as he removes each piece.

LOW PREP *Hammer Tees*

Materials:

- ☐ Golf Tees
- ☐ Plastic Hammer
- ☐ Playdough or a Styrofoam Block

Directions:

Ask your toddler if he would enjoy hammering. We used a Styrofoam block as our pretend wood block and golf tees as our nails. Styrofoam does start to crumble and make a mess, so playdough is also a good option. Place the tip of a golf tee into the Styrofoam block and ask your toddler to hammer the tee into the block. Once he has had practiced several times, let him place the tee on the block and hammer.

LOW PREP Thread Cereal

Materials:

- ☐ Fruit Loops or Cheerios
- ☐ Pipe Cleaner

Directions:

Ask your toddler if he wants to make a necklace or bracelet. Place one piece of cereal at the very end of the pipe cleaner, and then fold the pipe cleaner around the cereal so the cereal doesn't fall off as your toddler threads it. Let him hold the pipe cleaner as he places the cereal on the pipe cleaner. If this is too difficult for him, you can hold the pipe cleaner as he places the cereal on it. When he fills it up, fold both ends together to make a bracelet or necklace.

LOW PREP Nuts and Bolts

Materials:

- ☐ Bolts
- ☐ Nuts

Directions:

You will need to sit with your toddler during this activity to make sure no tiny pieces go in his mouth. You can gather a bunch of bolts and nuts from daddy's collection. Show your toddler how to twist the nut around the bolt. See if he can twist it all the way up to the top of the bolt. Next, he can work on untwisting the nut.

Cut Troll Hair

Materials:

- ☐ Toilet Paper Tube
- ☐ Marker
- ☐ Scissors
- ☐ Toddler Scissors

Directions:

You will need to get a toilet paper tube and draw a smiley face close to one end of the tube. Next, cut the other end of the tube into fringes just above the smiley face. The fringes should look like hair.

Ask your toddler if he would like to cut a troll's hair. Explain that he is only allowed to cut this troll's hair and not people's hair. Show him how to correctly hold scissors. Show him how to open and close the scissors. Now let him hold the troll's face with one hand while he cuts the hair with the other hand. Your toddler might want more than one troll's hair to cut.

Toilet Paper Tube Threading

Materials:

- ☐ 3 Toilet Paper Tubes
- ☐ 10+ Straws
- ☐ Single Hole Puncher

Directions:

Cut your toilet paper tubes in half. This should enable you to punch holes throughout the tube. Use the hole puncher to punch holes all around the toilet paper tubes.

Ask your toddler if he would like to play a game where he puts straws in the holes. Show him the tubes filled with holes. Next, show him how you can thread a straw through a hole on one side and another hole on the other side. Let him play with the tubes and straws.

LOW PREP Rubber Bands Around a Can

Materials:

- ☐ Can
- ☐ 10+ Rubber Bands

Directions:

Ask your toddler if he wants to see how many rubber bands will fit around a can. Place a regular can, like an unopened tomato sauce can, in front of your toddler. Hand your toddler a bunch of rubber bands. Show him how you stretch out the rubber band to place it around the can. Warn him that rubber bans can "snap back" and hurt, if he is not careful. Now let him do it. See how many rubber bands it takes to cover the can.

LOW PREP Tong Block Stack

Materials:

- ☐ Tongs
- ☐ Building Blocks

Directions:

Ask your toddler if he would enjoy building a tower using a special tool. Show him he can use the tongs to pick up a block, and then place the block on top of other blocks. See how tall of a tower he can build.

We have the foam building blocks so it was a little easier for my sons to pick the blocks up with the tongs. Wooden blocks may be a more difficult to pick up with tongs.

Gross Motor Activities

LOW PREP Ball Walk

Materials:

- ☐ 2 Bins
- ☐ Various Balls
- ☐ Big Spoon

Directions:

Ask your toddler if he would like to play a game. Place one bin on one side of the room and place the other bin on the other side of the room. Place all the balls in one bin. The balls can vary in size but should not be larger than your toddler can manage "transporting" with a spoon. Tell your toddler that he will place the ball on a spoon and attempt to carry it to the other bin and dump it in the bin. Encourage him to see how many steps he can take toward the bin while keeping the ball in the spoon.

LOW PREP Catch a Balloon

Materials:

- ☐ Balloon

Directions:

Ask your toddler if he would like to play catch. Let him pick a colored balloon. Blow it up and play a game of catch. This is a great way to work on hand-eye coordination because the balloon travels more slowly than a ball.

LOW PREP Walk the Line

Materials:

- ☐ Chalk

Directions:

Ask your toddler if he would like to go outside to play a fun walking game. Use a piece of chalk to draw a straight line, a zigzag line, a curvy line, and any other kind of lines you would like. Tell your toddler to walk on the line and try to only step on the line because if he steps off the line he will fall into the lava. It's quite fun to play the game with him!

Pom Pom Hockey

Materials:

- ☐ Pom Poms
- ☐ Broom(s)
- ☐ Tape

Directions:

Ask your toddler if he would like to play hockey. Use tape to create two squares on the floor. Tape the squares across the room from each other. These are the goals. Place all the pom poms between the goals. Tell your toddler which goal is his. Tell him he needs to use the broom as his hockey stick and shoot as many pom poms as he can into his goal. If you have two brooms, it's a lot of fun to compete against each other.

If you don't have brooms you can make a hockey stick using a cardboard tube from the center of wrapping paper, a paper plate, and tape. Cut a paper plate in half. Attach the plate to the tube with tape.

LOW PREP

Soccer Ball Obstacle Course

Materials:

- ☐ Toddler Soccer Ball
- ☐ Cones

Directions:

In your home or yard, set up an obstacle course for your toddler to kick a soccer ball. You can use cones, but if you don't have cones you can use items such as chairs, pillows, a trash can, a bike, the couch, etc.

Ask your toddler if he wants to go through an obstacle course. Show him how he will use his feet to kick the ball around each object.

Throw Ball at Targets

Materials:

- ☐ 5 Paper Plates
- ☐ Tape
- ☐ Marker
- ☐ Soft Ball

Directions:

Using five plates, number the plates one through five. Write each number really big on each plate. Tape the plates to a window or use sticky-tac to stick them to a wall.

Ask your toddler if he wants to play a fun throwing game. Demonstrate throwing the ball at a plate. Tell him that each plate has points on it and when he hits a plate he will receive the number of points written on the plate. Play with your toddler, and see who will be first to earn 10 points!

LOW PREP Stair Climb

Materials:

- ☐ 5 of His Favorite Toys
- ☐ Basket

Directions:

Ask your toddler if he would like to climb the stairs. Place his five favorite toys at the top of the stairs. Tell him he needs to climb the stairs to collect his toys. He can climb on his hands and knees or walk (with supervision). After picking up each toy, he will bring it back down the stairs and put it in the basket. Tell him he can scoot down the stairs on his bottom or walk (with supervision). Do this until all five toys are in the basket at the bottom of the stairs.

LOW PREP Walking on Pillows

Materials:

- ☐ A Bunch of Pillows

Directions:

Lay out a bunch of pillows in a line on the floor and ask your toddler if he wants to walk or jump across them. You can turn it into a game where he has to rescue a stuffed animal from one end of the pillow line and bring it back safely home at the other end.

Bubble Wrap Pop

Materials:

- ☐ Long Piece of Bubble Wrap
- ☐ Tape

Directions:

Tape a long piece of bubble wrap to the floor. You can tape one down for yourself too. Ask your toddler if he wants to play a racing game. Tell him the first person to pop all of the bubbles on the mat wins the game. He can jump, run, crawl, or leap to pop the bubbles.

Holiday Activities

New Year's Day Activities

Holiday Activities

About New Year's Day:

New Year's Day is celebrated on the first day of the new year. In the United States we use the Gregorian calendar. The start of our new year is on January 1st. Some people make New Year's resolutions, which are promises to do something better in the coming year.

LOW PREP New Year's I-Spy

Materials:

- ☐ New Year's I-Spy Activity Page (Appendix K)
- ☐ Crayons

Directions:

Ask your toddler if he would like to do a fun I-Spy game. Show him the *I-Spy* activity page. Show him the pictures at the bottom of the page. Tell him he will find these pictures on the *I-Spy* handout. Ask him to pick a crayon. Point to the clocks and ask your toddler to find all of the clocks on the *I-Spy* page. When he finds a clock, ask him to cross it out with his crayon. After he finds all of the clocks, have him count how many clocks he found and write the number beside the clock picture at the bottom of the page. You might need to help him write the number.

For the next set of pictures on the *I-Spy* activity page, have your little one choose a different colored crayon. Repeat the process he did with the clocks. Do this until he has found all of the pictures. Some toddlers, like my younger son, needed to take a break halfway through the activity, which is totally fine!

LOW PREP Confetti Eruption

Materials:

- ☐ Confetti or Glitter
- ☐ 1/3 Cup of Baking Soda
- ☐ Spoon
- ☐ Vinegar
- ☐ Plastic Party Glasses or Clear Cup
- ☐ Turkey Baster or Squirt Bottle
- ☐ Cookie Sheet

Directions:

Ask your toddler if he wants to make a New Year's eruption. Pour about 1/3 cup of baking soda into the clear cup. Ask your toddler to pour in some glitter, and mix it together with a spoon. Place the clear cup on a cookie sheet to help avoid a big mess to clean up. Pour some vinegar into a small bowl. Show your toddler how to squeeze the turkey baster to suck up the vinegar. Next, tell him he can squirt the vinegar into the cup. Be sure to watch the excitement in his face as the mixture erupts.

Make a Noise Maker

Materials:

- ☐ 2 Paper Plates
- ☐ Hot Glue Gun
- ☐ Dried Beans
- ☐ Craft Stick
- ☐ Paint, Glitter, Crayons, Jewels, etc.

Directions:

Ask your toddler if he would enjoy making a noise maker to celebrate the new year. Let your toddler decorate the two paper plates with paint, crayons, glitter, or whatever you have on hand. He will need to decorate the bottom of the plates. When he finishes decorating the plates, turn the plates over.

Ask your toddler to put a handful of dried beans on one plate. You will need to use the hot glue gun to glue the craft stick to the edge of the plate with beans. Place a ring of hot glue around the edge of the plate with beans, and then place the second plate on top of the glue. Press the edges together. Once the glue dries your little one can play with his noise maker. Your little one will have a blast with the noise maker, but you might get tired of all the noise—sorry!

Countdown Clock

Materials:

- ☐ Paper Plate
- ☐ Paint or Crayons
- ☐ Paintbrushes
- ☐ Brass Fastener
- ☐ Marker
- ☐ Construction Paper
- ☐ Scissors

Directions:

Ask your toddler if he would like to make a clock to help countdown to the new year. First, he will need to paint or color the bottom of a paper plate. Let it dry. Using construction paper, cut out two clock hands. If your toddler has used scissors before, draw the clock hands on the construction paper and let him cut them out. It's ok if they aren't perfect. It's good to let your toddler practice his cutting skills. My 4 year old cut out the clock hands himself, but I cut out the clock hands for my 2 year old. Be sure to make one clock hand longer than the other. Use the brass fastener to secure the clock hands to the center of the plate.

Let your toddler write the clock numbers. I made dotted numbers for my 2 year old to trace. I drew a line where my 4 year old needed to write each number.

LOW PREP Year Dots

Materials:

- ☐ Paper
- ☐ Marker
- ☐ Do-a-Dot Markers

Directions:

Ask your toddler if he would like to use Do-a-Dot markers. Using large numbers, write out the year, 20__, on a piece of paper. Next, have your toddler trace the numbers using the Do-a-Dot markers. This is a good prewriting skills activity.

If you don't have Do-a-Dot markers, you can use a clothes pin to hold a cotton ball. Q-tips are also a great substitute for Do-a-Dot markers.

Martin Luther King Jr. Day Activities

About Martin Luther King Jr. Day:

Dr. Martin Luther King Jr. was a famous Civil Rights leader and pastor in the 1950s and 60s. At this time, people were separated by the color of their skin. Dr. King led many peaceful protests in an attempt to end the separation. He gave his famous, "I Have a Dream" speech in 1963.

Egg Activity

Materials:

- ☐ Martin Luther King Jr. Activity Page (Appendix L)
- ☐ Crayons
- ☐ White Egg
- ☐ Brown Egg
- ☐ 2 Bowls

Directions:

Ask your toddler if he would like to learn about Dr. Martin Luther King Jr. Show your toddler the white egg and brown egg. Talk about how the eggs are the same and different. Have your toddler draw the outside of the two eggs on the activity page. Let him trace the letters to spell "different." Ask your toddler what he thinks the inside of each egg looks like. Crack each egg open in its own bowl and let your toddler see how they are the same on the inside. Now he can draw a picture of what the inside of the eggs looked like, and complete the rest of the activity page.

Talk to your little one about what equality means and how even though people might look different they should still be treated the same. Tell your child, "Our goal as a family is to treat everyone with respect and kindness."

LOW PREP Shape Graph

Materials:

- ☐ I Have a Dream Activity Page (Appendix M)
- ☐ Do-a-Dot Markers or Q-tips and Paint

Directions:

Ask your toddler if he would like to do a shape activity. Show him the *I Have a Dream* activity page and remind him about how Dr. Martin Luther King Jr. gave a speech saying he had a dream that everyone would be nice to each other. Ask him to find all of the stars on the page. When he finds a star, ask him to put a dot on it. After finding all of the stars, ask him to count how many stars he found. Explain that since he found __ stars, he will need to make __dots at the bottom of the page.

He should follow these same steps for the other three shapes. After his graph is filled in, see if he can tell you which shape had the most boxes filled in and which had the least.

Valentine's Day Activities

Holiday Activities

About Valentine's Day:

Valentine's Day celebrates love. It is celebrated on February 14th. People celebrate by sending the people they love cards, candy, or flowers. No one is sure where Valentine's Day originated. There are a few St. Valentine's from the early Catholic church from which the day could have been named.

Heart Lacing

Materials:

- ☐ Construction Paper
- ☐ Scissors
- ☐ Marker
- ☐ Single Hole Puncher
- ☐ Yarn

Directions:

Ask your toddler if he would like to lace a heart. You will need to draw a big heart on construction paper, and then cut it out. Punch holes around the edge of the heart. Use your marker to label the holes.

You can punch more holes for older toddlers and label the holes with more numbers than a younger child. For my four year old, I fit 20 holes around the edge of the heart and labeled the holes 1-20. For my two year old, I punched 10 holes around the edge of the heart and labeled the holes with numbers 1-10.

Tie a long piece of yarn to the first hole. I put a piece of tape around the other end of the yarn to prevent it from unraveling while they lace. Tell your toddler to put the piece of yarn through the number two hole. Tell him to find the next number and keep going until he is finished. You can also label the holes with letters.

LOW PREP Heart Patterns

Materials:

- ☐ Heart Pattern Activity Page (Appendix N)
- ☐ Candy Hearts

Directions:

Ask your toddler if he would like to make patterns with candy hearts. Show him the *Heart Pattern* activity page. You might want to cut the patterns into separate strips so it's easier for your toddler to focus on one pattern at a time. Show him the first pattern. Say the pattern to him as you point to each heart. Ask him to say the pattern with you. Then ask him if he knows what color comes next in the pattern. Let your toddler place the correct candy heart on the pattern. Say the pattern again with your toddler and ask them if they know what color would come next. Let them place the correct candy heart on the pattern. I would let them add three candy hearts to the pattern and then move to the next pattern.

Fizzing Hearts

Materials:

- ☐ Poster Board
- ☐ Marker
- ☐ Scissors
- ☐ Baking Soda
- ☐ Vinegar
- ☐ Food Coloring
- ☐ Spoons
- ☐ Eye Droppers
- ☐ Pan
- ☐ Muffin Pan

Directions:

Ask your toddler if he would like to make a fizzing heart. Cut out a heart from poster board. Use half a piece of poster board for one heart. Place the heart on a baking pan to help contain the mess. Next, ask your toddler to use a spoon to spread baking soda all over the heart. Ask your little one to pick four colors of food coloring.

While he picks the colors, fill four cups on the muffin pan with vinegar. Fill each cup approximately half full. Put a few drops of each food coloring in the separate muffin cups. Put a spoon or eye dropper in each color. Let your toddler use the spoon or eye dropper to color the heart from the colored liquid you made in the muffin cups. It will start to fizz and spread. Let your little one fill the heart with color. It should look like a tie-dyed heart when he is finished. When he finishes, let it dry. After it dries, dust off the baking soda and it's ready for your toddler to write a special Valentine's message!

Heart Number Match

Materials:

- ☐ Heart Number Match Activity Page (Appendix O)
- ☐ Scissors

Directions:

Ask your toddler if he would like to match hearts together. You will need to cut out the hearts from the *Heart Number Match* activity page. Cut the hearts in half and place all of the numerical heart halves together and all of the dotted heart halves together. Ask your toddler to pick a heart half from the dotted pile. Ask him to count how many dots there are on the heart half. You can help him if he needs it. Ask him to find the numerical heart half that matches the dot heart half. Place them together to make a whole heart.

For example, if your toddler picks up the heart half with five dots, ask him to count the dots. When he says there are five dots on the heart half, you can ask him to find the number five heart half. When he finds it, let him put it together. Do this for all of the numbers.

Heart Hunt

Materials:

- ☐ Construction Paper
- ☐ Scissors

Directions:

Cut out 10 small (4 inch) hearts from construction paper. You can cut them out from the same colored paper or different colors. Hide them around your house. Ask your toddler if he would like to go on a hunt for hearts. Tell your little one that you hid 10 hearts around the house and he needs to find them. Ask him to bring each heart to you as he finds it.

President's Day Activities

Holiday Activities

About President's Day:

President's Day honors two great Presidents, George Washington and Abraham Lincoln. It is celebrated the third Monday in February. It is celebrated during this time because George Washington's Birthday is February 22 and Abraham Lincoln's is February 12.

George Washington Color by Number

Materials:

- ☐ George Washington Color by Number Activity Page (Appendix P)
- ☐ Crayons

Directions:

Ask your toddler if he would like to color a picture of George Washington. Tell him that this is a different kind of coloring page because he needs to color the number with the right color. I'd start by showing him what each number is supposed to be colored. You can highlight the color word with the corresponding crayon.

Next, ask your little one to find a number one on the George Washington picture and color it black. When he finishes, ask him if there are anymore number ones on the picture to color. When he finishes coloring all of the ones, have him color the number twos the correct color, and so on. When he finishes, he can hang his picture on the refrigerator.

Make a Log Cabin

Materials:

- ☐ 6 or 7 Craft Sticks
- ☐ Construction Paper (Brown and Another Piece)
- ☐ Scissors
- ☐ Glue
- ☐ A Penny
- ☐ Crayons

Directions:

Ask your little one if he would like to make Abraham Lincoln's log cabin. Ask him to pick out a piece of construction paper to glue the log cabin on. Have him glue the craft sticks on the construction paper—you'll want to glue them horizontally stacked to form a square.

Draw a triangle roof, rectangle door, and square window on the brown piece of construction paper. If your little one is not skilled with scissors, cut out the roof, door, and window. If your toddler would like to try to cut these out, let him try. Once cut out, have your toddler glue the roof, window, and door onto the log cabin.

Hand your little one the penny and show him the picture of Abraham Lincoln. Next, let your toddler glue the penny onto the window of the log cabin. Your little one can now use crayons to add a sun, clouds, trees, etc. to his picture.

St. Patrick's Day Activities

Holiday Activities

About St. Patrick's Day:

St. Patrick's Day is celebrated on March 17th each year. It celebrates a Christian saint named Patrick. Patrick was a missionary who helped bring Christianity to Ireland. The day generally celebrates Irish culture and heritage.

LOW PREP Green Scavenger Hunt

Materials:

- ☐ Green Scavenger Hunt Activity Page (Appendix Q)
- ☐ Green Crayon

Directions:

Ask your toddler if he wants to go on a scavenger hunt for green things. You can read the items to your toddler one at a time off the *Green Scavenger Hunt* activity page. When he finds each item let him cross it off the list with a green crayon.

Clover Sort

Materials:

- ☐ Clover Activity Page (Appendix R)
- ☐ Piece of Paper
- ☐ Marker
- ☐ Scissors

Directions:

Turn your piece of paper to landscape (the longer sides of the paper form the top and bottom of the page) and draw two lines from top to bottom dividing the paper into three columns. At the top of the first column draw a circle and write the word "Circle." At the top of the second column draw a square and write the word "Square." At the top of the third column draw a triangle and write the word "Triangle." Next, cut out the clovers from the *Clover Sort* activity page. Mix them up.

Ask your toddler if he would like to sort some clovers. Show him the different clovers. Show him that all of the circle clovers go in the first column, all of the square clovers go in the second column, and all of the triangle clovers go in the third column. Let him pick up a clover and ask him what shape is on the clover, then ask him where it will go. Let him place all of the clovers on the chart.

One other activity you can do with the clovers is to ask your toddler to sort the clover sets from biggest to smallest or vice versa.

Fruit Loop Rainbow

Materials:

- ☐ Paper
- ☐ Crayons/Markers/Colored Pencils
- ☐ Fruit Loops

Directions:

Draw a rainbow on a piece of paper. The stripes should be thick enough for your little one to place a fruit loop on each colored stripe. You will need a red, orange, yellow, green, blue, and purple stripe.

Ask your little one if he would like to make a rainbow out of fruit loops. Pour some fruit loops in a bowl and let your little one place fruit loops on the correct colored stripe until the rainbow is full.

If your little one needs a challenge you can have him roll a die to see how many fruit loops to place on each stripe. For example, if the total from the die was the number three, he would place three red fruit loops on the red stripe. Your toddler could do the same for each colored stripe. He would continue until the rainbow is completely covered in fruit loops.

LOW PREP Color Mixing

Materials:

- ☐ Red, Blue, and Yellow Paint
- ☐ 3 Pieces of Paper
- ☐ 3 Paintbrushes

Directions:

Ask your little one if he would enjoy mixing paint together in an attempt to create a new color! Place a piece of paper in front of your toddler. Place a small glob of red paint on the paper and a small glob of yellow paint on the paper. Ask your toddler to use the paintbrush or his finger to mix the colors together to discover what new color they can make. Repeat this activity using yellow and blue, and red and blue.

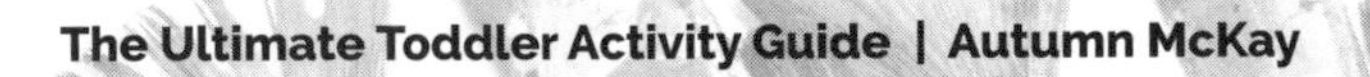

LOW PREP Shamrock Stamping

Materials:

- ☐ Green Paint
- ☐ Paper Plate
- ☐ Jumbo Marshmallow
- ☐ Paintbrush
- ☐ Paper

Directions:

Ask your toddler if he would like to make shamrocks by stamping. Ask your little one to pick out a piece of paper. Squirt some green paint onto a paper plate. Show your toddler how to make a shamrock by stamping the marshmallow side by side and then once over the two circles (like an upside-down Mickey Mouse). Let your little one fill the page with as many shamrocks as he would like. Now he can use a paintbrush to paint a small stem for each shamrock.

Easter Activities

Holiday Activities

About Easter:

Easter celebrates Jesus rising from the grave. The Friday before Easter, Good Friday, is the day Jesus died on the cross. Leaders in Jerusalem did not like Jesus because he claimed to be the Son of God. So the Roman leader, Pilate, decided to have Jesus crucified, but after three days Jesus rose from the grave.

There are also some other Easter traditions that include the Easter bunny hiding eggs for children to find.

Resurrection Eggs

Materials:

- ☐ Resurrection Eggs Activity Page (Appendix S)
- ☐ 6 Easter Eggs
- ☐ Marker
- ☐ Heart Sticker or Cut Out
- ☐ Band Aid
- ☐ Cross Sticker or Cut Out
- ☐ Rock
- ☐ Piece of Gauze or Cloth
- ☐ Half of Egg Carton

Directions:

Before the activity you will need to fill the plastic eggs and place them in the egg carton. Write E-A-S-T-E-R on the outside of the eggs—one letter for each egg. Place the heart in the first "E" egg. Place a band-aid in the "A" egg. Place a cross in the "S" egg. Place a rock in the "T" egg. Place the gauze in the second "E" egg. And leave the "R" egg empty. Now you are ready to begin the activity.

Ask your toddler if he would like to learn about why we celebrate Easter. Show him the egg carton with the eggs in it. Ask him to open the first "E" egg. Ask him what is in the egg. Next, read the "E" statement from the *Resurrection Eggs* activity page to him. Do this for each of the eggs. My sons loved doing this activity and hearing the story. We did it at least three times a day during Easter week.

Easter Egg Counting

Materials:

- ☐ 10 or More Plastic Eggs
- ☐ Marker

Directions:

Split the 10 eggs in half. On the bottom half of the eggs write the numbers 1-10; one number for each bottom half. On the top half of each egg draw dots for each number. For example, for the egg half having the number four on it, you will draw four dots on the top half of the egg.

If you would like to make it a little more challenging for your little one, you can make sure that the top and bottom half colors do not match. Another challenging activity would be to match numbers to number words.

Ask your little one if he would enjoy an Easter egg counting game. Explain to him that he will pick out an egg half with dots marked on it and count the dots. Next, tell him to find an egg half with the number that matches how many dots he counted. He should then connect the matching top and bottom halves. For example, if he picked up a top half with six dots, he will first count the dots. After counting the dots (in this case six) he will search for the bottom half of the egg that has the number six on it. Once found, he connects the matching halves together.

Easter Eggercises

Materials:

- ☐ 12 Plastic Eggs
- ☐ 12 Strips of Paper
- ☐ Pen

Directions:

On your strips of paper you will need to write the exercises your toddler will do. You can write:

1 somersault

2 pencil rolls

3 giant leaps

4 ninja kicks

5 frog hops

6 huge steps

7 bunny hops

8 steps backwards

9 donkey kicks

10 jumping jacks

11 steps sideways

12 soldier marches

After writing out the exercises, fold and place one strip in each egg. Place the eggs in a basket. Ask your toddler if he would like to do some fun exercises. Have him pick an egg from the basket and open it. Read the strip to him. Do the exercise with him. Place the egg to the side and have your little one pick another egg from the basket. Do this until all the exercises are done. This is a great way for you to workout while your child is burning off some energy!

Sink or Float Eggs

Materials:

- ☐ Plastic Easter Eggs
- ☐ Odd Objects that will Fit inside the Eggs (pennies, cotton balls, paper clips, Cheerios, etc.)
- ☐ Bowl of Water

Directions:

Ask your toddler if he would like to do an experiment to discover if his Easter eggs will sink or float. Ask him to help you find some small objects that would fit inside an Easter egg. Show him an example of pennies fitting inside the egg. Collect six to ten items. Let your toddler help you place the items inside the eggs—one item for each egg. Now fill a bowl with water. Let your little one pick an egg to place in the water to see if it will sink or float. Let the egg sit on the water for a little bit to see what it will do. Ask your toddler if the egg is floating or sinking.

In one of our eggs we put one penny. This egg floated on top of the water. I asked my sons what they thought would happen if we put more pennies in the egg. One said, "I don't know" and one said, "It will float." So, we tried adding more pennies to see what would happen. They thought it was cool that it now sank.

Disappearing Eggshell Experiment

Materials:

- ☐ 16oz Mason Jar with Lid
- ☐ White Vinegar
- ☐ Fresh Egg

Directions:

Ask your little one if he would like to try to make the shell from an egg disappear. Let your toddler feel the hard egg. Let him place the egg gently into the mason jar. Now let him pour the vinegar into the jar. You can help. You will need to leave half an inch of space from the top of the jar. Put the lid on the jar. Make sure it's not too tight so that the gas can escape the jar. Let it sit for about two days, and then you can remove the egg from the jar and rinse it with water. Let your little one touch it and feel it. Ask him if it feels different from when he first held it.

Earth Day Activities

Holiday Activities

About Earth Day:

Earth Day is celebrated on April 22nd each year. It was founded by U.S. Senator Gaylord Nelson. He hoped the day would raise awareness for our environment and heighten concern for our trees, air, animals, and water.

Recycle Sorting

Materials:

- ☐ Recycle Sorting Activity Page (Appendix T)
- ☐ Scissors
- ☐ Glue

Directions:

Tell your little one there are certain items we can throw away in the trash and certain items we can recycle. Recycle means using things that have already been used to make new things. For example, a newspaper can be recycled and made into a new birthday card. Explain to your little one that you can recycle things like paper, plastic and cardboard. You can't recycle things like food, Styrofoam, or sunglasses; those things are thrown away in the trash.

Show your little one the *Recycle Sorting* activity page. Ask him to cut out the 10 pictures at the bottom of the page. If he cannot use scissors, cut the pictures out yourself. Hold up each picture and ask him if he can recycle it, or if he needs to throw it in the trash. (Answer Key: Recycle-newspaper, box, plastic bottle, cereal box, magazine. Trash-food, Styrofoam to go container, sunglasses, pet food bag, glass pan.) Now ask him to glue the picture in the correct box. Do this for all 10 pictures.

LOW PREP Make a Bird Feeder

Materials:

- ☐ Toilet Paper Tube
- ☐ Peanut Butter
- ☐ Plate
- ☐ Birdseed
- ☐ Knife
- ☐ String

Directions:

Ask your toddler if he would like to make a bird feeder. Tell him you are recycling a toilet paper tube by using it for something new—a bird feeder. If age appropriate, let him use a knife (we used butter knives) to spread peanut butter on the toilet paper tube. This will probably be somewhat messy. Spread some bird seed onto a plate and let your little one roll the peanut butter covered tube across the bird seed so that the bird seed sticks to the tube. Thread a piece of string through the tube and tie a knot in the ends. Now you can take your little one outside to help him find a spot to hang his bird feeder. We hung our bird feeders close to a window so we could watch the birds come eat.

4th of July Activities

Holiday Activities

About 4th of July:

The 4th of July is America's birthday. July 4, 1776 is the day America signed the Declaration of Independence, announcing its liberation from England.

Make a Flag Waffle

Materials:

- ☐ Waffle
- ☐ Whipped Cream
- ☐ Sliced Strawberries
- ☐ Blueberries

Directions:

Ask your toddler if he would like to make a waffle into an American flag. You can either make homemade waffles together with your toddler or you can cheat, like me, and heat up a frozen waffle in the toaster.

Once your waffles are ready, ask your toddler to place blueberries into the holes of the upper left-hand quadrant of the waffle. Next, ask him to make horizontal stripes with the sliced strawberries, starting at the top of the upper right quadrant of the waffle. Leave space in between the strawberry stripes for whipped cream. We placed four stripes of strawberries. Now ask your toddler to either spray or scoop whipped cream stripes onto the waffle in between the strawberry stripes. Enjoy your tasty flag!

LOW PREP

American Flag Dot to Dot

Materials:

- ☐ American Flag Dot to Dot Activity Page (Appendix U)
- ☐ Crayons

Directions:

Ask your toddler if he would enjoy coloring an American flag. Show him the *American Flag Dot to Dot* activity page. Explain that he is going to draw a line to connect the dots, but that he has to go in order of the letters. Tell him to put his crayon on the letter A, and then ask him to find the letter B. When he finds it, tell him to draw a line from the "A" dot to the "B" dot. Now ask him if he can find the "C" dot. When he finds it, ask him to draw a line from the "B" dot to the "C" dot.

Continue asking him to find the next dot until the end, or if your toddler feels comfortable enough, let him try to finish the activity page by himself. When he finishes connecting the dots ask him if he would like to color the flag. You can tell him what colors are on the American flag, but let him use his creativity to color this one.

Fireworks Painting

Materials:

- ☐ Paint
- ☐ Construction Paper
- ☐ 3 Paper Plates
- ☐ 3 Toilet Paper Tubes
- ☐ Scissors

Directions:

See if your little one would like to paint fireworks. You need at least three toilet paper tubes. Cut the toilet paper tube into a lot of 2-inch-long fringes. After they are cut, push it against the table so the fringes lay flat against the table. Ask your toddler to pick out a piece of construction paper and three colors of paint for the fireworks. Squirt a thin layer of paint onto separate paper plates. Place one toilet paper tube, fringe side down, into each paint color. Now your little one can take the tube and stamp it onto his paper to create fireworks.

LOW PREP *Flag Fingerprint Painting*

Materials:

- ☐ American Flag Activity Page (Appendix V)
- ☐ Paint or Do-a-Dot Markers

Directions:

Ask your toddler if he would like to count how many stars are on the American flag. Show him the *American Flag* activity page and explain that he is going to count and paint the numbers on the flag. You can use Do-a-Dot markers for less mess, or you can let your little one dip his finger in the paint.

Tell him to dip his finger in white paint and stamp the star as he says the number. Counting to fifty is a lot for a toddler but it is good for your toddler to see and hear the numbers. After he finishes counting the stars he can dip his finger in red paint and count the numbers on the stripes. Ask him to stamp the number as he says it.

LOW PREP *M&M Graphing*

Materials:

- ☐ M&M Graphing Activity Page (Appendix W)
- ☐ M&Ms

Directions:

Ask your toddler if he would like to do an activity with M&Ms. You will need to buy "4th of July" M&Ms. If you can't find them, look for "4th of July" marshmallows.

Show your little one the activity page and give him a small bowl of the M&Ms. Explain that he will place all the blue M&Ms in the blue column, all the red M&Ms in the red column, and all the white M&Ms in the white column. You might want to place each colored M&M in the correct column to show him how to do it.

After he has placed all of the M&Ms ask him which color has the most and which color has the least. You might have to explain what most and least mean. You can also ask him to count how many M&Ms are in each column.

Columbus Day Activities

About Columbus Day:

Columbus Day celebrates that Christopher Columbus arrived in the Americas. In 1492, Christopher Columbus sailed from Spain across the ocean in the Nina, Pinta, and Santa Maria to discover new land.

LOW PREP Handprint Boat

Materials:

- ☐ Blue Construction Paper
- ☐ Blue, Brown and White Paint
- ☐ Paper Plate
- ☐ Paintbrushes

Directions:

Ask your toddler if he would like to make a boat like Christopher Columbus sailed. Ask your little one to paint the bottom half of his paper blue to be the ocean. When he finishes painting the ocean, paint the palm of his hand brown. Guide him in pressing his hand down, right above the ocean, so it will look like a boat is floating on the sea. After you clean your little one's hand, instruct him to paint a square sail over each of the three middle fingers using white paint. He can also paint some clouds in the sky. Once his painting dries, you can find a place to hang it.

Make a Spy Glass

Materials:

- ☐ Paper Cup (the bottom of the cup needs to be bigger than a toilet paper tube)
- ☐ Toilet Paper Tube
- ☐ Paint
- ☐ Paper Plate
- ☐ Paintbrush
- ☐ Construction Paper
- ☐ Scissors
- ☐ Glue

Directions:

Ask your little one if he would like to make a spy glass like Christopher Columbus would have used to look out across the ocean. You can even show him a picture of one. First, you will need to ask your toddler to paint the toilet paper tube and cup. Let him select the colors. Let it dry.

Once they are dry place the toilet paper roll on top of the bottom of the cup. Trace around the tube. Cut out the circle you traced. Now make a ring out of construction paper. Place the bottom of your cup on the paper and let your toddler trace around it. Place the toilet paper tube in the center of the tracing and ask your toddler to trace around the tube. Cut out the ring. Place glue on one end of the toilet paper tube, and ask your toddler to place the ring on top of the glue. The ring will help the tube from sliding out of the cup. Once the glue is dry, insert the toilet paper tube into the hole in the cup. Insert it so that the ring is on the inside of the cup. Now your little one can look around at different things.

Halloween Activities

Holiday Activities

About Halloween:

People called the Celts had a festival in honor of souls of the past. The Roman Empire conquered the Celts and took over this tradition. The Romans spread this idea to a lot of the world that on the last day of October the souls of the past come to visit.

People typically celebrate Halloween by dressing up in costumes, carving pumpkins, and going trick or treating.

LOW PREP Make a Spider Web

Materials:

- ☐ Paper Plate
- ☐ Single Hole Puncher
- ☐ Black Crayon
- ☐ Yarn
- ☐ Tape (optional)

Directions:

Ask your little one if he would like to make a spider web. Let your little one draw a spider on the paper plate using the black crayon. You can explain how to draw a spider by telling him to draw a circle and eight legs, or just let him use his creativity. Ask your toddler to help you punch holes around the edge of the paper plate.

Cut a piece of yarn three feet. Tie one end of yarn around one of the holes on the plate. Wrap a piece of tape around the other end of the yarn to keep it from fraying as your toddler threads it through the holes. Tell your toddler that he can put the string through any hole he wants. You might need to show him how to thread it. When he is finished, tie the end to a hole so that it doesn't come apart.

Pumpkin Catapult

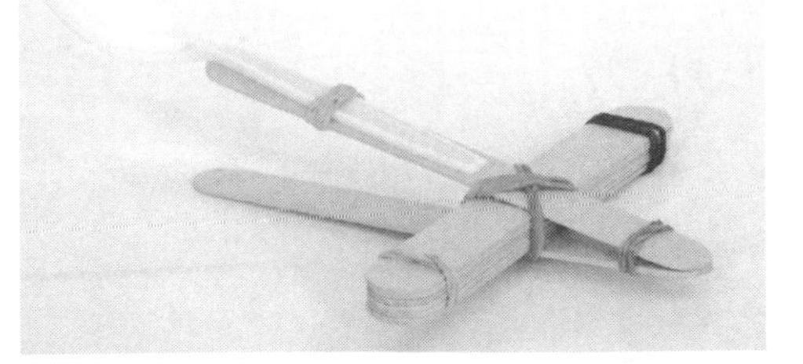

Materials:

- ☐ 8-12 Craft Sticks
- ☐ Pumpkin Candies
- ☐ 6 Rubber Bands
- ☐ Plastic Spoon

Directions:

Ask your toddler if he would like to make pumpkins fly through the air. Make a stack of craft sticks (about six) and wrap a rubber band around each end. Take two additional craft sticks and stack them together. Wrap a rubber band around one end—this end will be the front of the catapult. Lay the two craft sticks flat on the table. Pull the two craft sticks slightly apart and slide the larger stack of craft sticks in between the two towards the rubber band; the larger stack will be perpendicular to the two craft sticks. . Now wrap a rubber band around both stacks where they meet—you might need two rubber bands for this. I wrapped the rubber bands diagonal to form an X where the two stacks met. Now place the plastic spoon handle on the top craft stick, and wrap a rubber band around the spoon handle and craft stick.

Ask your toddler to place a pumpkin candy on the spoon. Hold the catapult down with one hand and show your toddler how to pull the spoon back. Let it go and see how far the pumpkin flies! You can try a different amount of craft sticks in the first stack to see if it makes the pumpkins fly further.

Ghost Matching

Materials:

- ☐ White Construction Paper
- ☐ Crayons

Directions:

Draw eight ghost outlines on a piece of white construction paper. Each ghost outline should be a different color. You can pick colors like red, blue, yellow, green, orange, purple, brown, pink, or black. In the center of the ghost, color a small square the same color as the outline—this is optional and only recommended if your toddler is new to colors.

Ask your little one if he would like to color some ghosts. Show him the ghosts you drew. Ask him the color of each ghost. Lay the same colored crayons that you used in front of your toddler. Tell him he needs to match the crayon to the correct colored ghost, so he can color the ghost the right color and make the ghost happy.

LOW PREP Pumpkin Hole Punch

Materials:

- ☐ Pumpkin Hole Punch Activity Page (Appendix X)
- ☐ Single Hole Puncher

Directions:

You will need the *Pumpkin Hole Punch* activity page. Cut the pumpkin out. Tell your toddler he will be able to punch holes into the pumpkin, but he will need to find the right number to hole punch. Help him find the number "1", and then let him punch a hole in the number. Ask him what comes after the number "1." After he responds with the correct answer, ask him to find the number "2" and so on. If he is unfamiliar with his numbers, please encourage and assist him.

LOW PREP Toilet Paper Mummies

Materials:

- ☐ Toilet Paper

Directions:

Ask your little one if he would like to be wrapped up like a mummy. You can use toilet paper to wrap your little one all the way up from head to toe. You can turn it into a fun game where you see how much of your toddler you can wrap in one minute.

Veterans Day Activities

About Veterans Day:

Veterans Day is celebrated on November 11th. It is a day we honor those that served in the United States Armed Forces.

Shape Soldier

Materials:

- ☐ Brown, White, and Black Construction Paper
- ☐ Green Do-a-Dot Marker or Paint
- ☐ Glue Stick
- ☐ Crayons

Directions:

Ask your toddler if he would like to make a soldier. If your little one is good at using scissors have him cut out the pieces. Cut the brown piece of construction paper in half, across the width of the paper. One of the rectangles will be the body of the soldier. Take the other half of the brown construction paper and cut four even strips, two inches thick, for the arms and legs. You should still have enough of the brown construction paper left to cut out a trapezoid for the helmet. Now, cut out a big circle for the head from the white construction paper. Cut out two small ovals from the white construction paper for hands. Cut out two small ovals from the black construction paper for the boots.

Ask your toddler to take the green Do-a-Dot marker and dot all of the brown shapes so that it will look like camouflage. Once it dries, you can start the assembly. Ask your toddler to find the big rectangle—this is the body. Ask him to find the big white circle. Place the circle at the top of the rectangle and glue it on—this is the head. Now ask him to find the trapezoid. Glue the trapezoid on top of the head to be the helmet. Ask your little one to find two long rectangles. Glue these to the sides of the body to be the arms. Ask your little one to find two white ovals. Let your toddler glue these to the ends of the arms to be the hands. Ask your toddler to find two more long rectangles and glue them to the bottom of the body to be the legs. And lastly, ask your toddler to find two black ovals to glue to the legs for the boots. When complete, your little one can draw a face on their soldier.

LOW PREP

Poppy Collage

Materials:

- ☐ Poppy Activity Page (Appendix Y)
- ☐ Red and Black Construction Paper
- ☐ Glue

Directions:

Tell your little one poppies are a flower that helps us to remember those who protect our country. Ask him if he would like to make a poppy collage. Have him tear the red and black construction paper into small pieces. Instruct him to take his glue and spread it all over the center of the poppy and place the small pieces of black construction paper in the center of the poppy. Spread glue on the petals and place the red pieces of paper on the petals. When he has finished you can find a nice place to hang it up.

Thanksgiving Activities

About Thanksgiving:

Thanksgiving is a day to give thanks for all the good things in your life. It started with the Pilgrims who settled at Plymouth, Massachusetts. They held the celebration to show thanks for their harvest in 1621.

Paper Plate Turkey

Materials:

- ☐ Paper Plate
- ☐ Construction Paper
- ☐ Scissors
- ☐ Glue
- ☐ Crayons
- ☐ Paint or Do-a-Dot Markers

Directions:

You will need to cut out some feathers for your toddler's paper plate turkey. Cut out as many as you would like and any color you would like. Write a number on each feather. I wrote numbers 1-6 for my two year old to practice, and numbers 12-18 for my four year old to practice. Go ahead and glue the feathers on the edge of the paper plate and give the glue time to dry.

Ask your toddler if he would like to help you count the feathers on a turkey. First, let him use crayons to color the body of the turkey and draw a face on the turkey. Show him the feathers have different numbers on them. Count the numbers together. Now explain that he will use his Do-a-Dot marker to put the same number of dots as the number on the feather. For example, on the number two feather he will put two dots. If you don't have Do-a-Dot markers, you can use paint and a q-tip.

LOW PREP Turkey Lunch

Materials:

- ☐ Sandwich Ingredients
- ☐ 2 M&Ms or Blueberries
- ☐ 1 Triangle Cheese Beak
- ☐ 8 Apple Slices
- ☐ Knife

Directions:

Ask your little one if he wants to make his sandwich into a turkey for lunch. Let him help you make a sandwich using whatever ingredients he likes best. My sons love peanut butter and jelly! Let your toddler help you cut his sandwich into a circle. Place two eyes, M&Ms or blueberries, in the middle of the sandwich. Cut out a tiny triangle from a piece of cheese to use as the turkey beak. Place the beak under the eyes.

Now slice up some apples. You can use two different colored apples to make it more fun. Let your little one place the apple slices around the top edge of the sandwich to be the feathers. Now he can enjoy his fun lunch.

Make a Pilgrim Hat

Materials:

- ☐ Pilgrim Hat Template Activity Page (Appendix Z)
- ☐ Scissors
- ☐ Glue
- ☐ Black, Yellow, and White Construction Paper
- ☐ Stapler

Directions:

Cut out the pieces from the *Pilgrim Hat Template* activity page. Ask your toddler if he would like to make a pilgrim hat. Place the pilgrim hat onto a piece of black construction paper. Let your toddler help you trace around the pilgrim hat template. Place the buckle onto a piece of yellow construction paper. Let your toddler help you trace around the buckle. Place your band on a piece of white construction paper. Let your toddler help you trace around the band. Now you will need to cut out each piece. Then, your toddler can glue the white band onto the hat. Finally, your toddler can glue the buckle onto the center of the band.

Cut out two or three strips, lengthwise, from the white construction paper. Staple two of the white strips together. Place the stapled white strips around your toddler's head. It should extend around the head, with a two inch overlap. If needed, add length by stapling the third strip of white construction paper to the other two strips already stapled together. Staple one end of the long strips to the back of the hat, and place the hat on your toddler's head to see where to staple the other end of the strip to the other side of the hat. Now your little one can wear their hat.

Paper Bag Turkey

Materials:

- ☐ Paper Lunch Bag
- ☐ Feathers
- ☐ White, Orange, and Red Construction Paper
- ☐ Glue
- ☐ Hot Glue Gun
- ☐ Scissors
- ☐ Marker or Crayon

Directions:

Ask your little one if he would like to make a turkey puppet. Ask him to pick out 10 feathers. Lay the paper bag on the table with the flap face down and the opening of the bag towards you. Use the hot glue gun to glue the feathers to the top of the bag. Tell your little one you will need to glue the feathers on the bag because this glue gets really hot. Ask him to hand you the feathers to glue. When you finish gluing the feathers, turn the bag over.

Now your toddler can make the turkey face. Cut out two white circles for eyes. Let your toddler glue them at the top of the flap. Cut out an orange beak and have your toddler glue it under the eyes. Cut out a red gobbler. Let your toddler glue it beside the beak. Now your toddler can color two black dots on the white circles to finish the eyes.

Help your toddler write a sentence about something he is thankful for on the body of the turkey. It's a good idea to share what thankful means and give him a few examples of ways you are thankful.

LOW PREP Thanksgiving Maze

Materials:

- ☐ Thanksgiving Maze Activity Page (Appendix AA)
- ☐ Crayon

Directions:

Ask your little one if he would enjoy helping the pilgrim find his turkey that is lost in the woods. Show him the *Thanksgiving Maze* activity page. Tell him he needs to help the pilgrim find his way to the turkey, but he can only go through paths that are open and not closed. Point to a closed off path. Let your little one go through the maze with his finger first. If he becomes "lost in the maze" have him start over and try a different path. After your child has discovered the correct path through the maze with his finger, let him use a crayon to draw his way through the maze.

Christmas Activities

About Christmas:

Christmas celebrates the birth of Jesus. It is on December 25th. Jesus is the son of God and was born to Mary and Joseph in the city of Bethlehem.

People often decorate their homes with lights and Christmas trees.

Jesus in a Manger

Materials:

- ☐ Paper Plate
- ☐ Crayons
- ☐ Scissors
- ☐ Yellow Tissue Paper
- ☐ Glue
- ☐ Yellow and White Construction Paper

Directions:

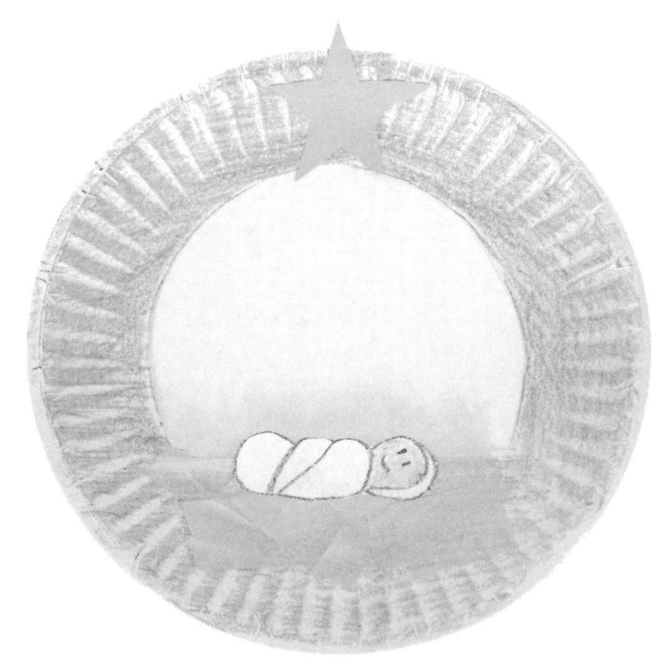

Ask your little one if he would like to make baby Jesus lying in a manger. You will need to cut out ¾ of the center circle of the plate. Cut out a star from your yellow construction paper. Let your little one draw a picture of baby Jesus on white construction paper, and then cut it out so it can go in the manger. Now let your toddler color the paper plate brown. When he is finished, let him spread glue on the center of the plate. Place strips of yellow tissue paper on the glue. Rub glue on the baby Jesus and stick the baby Jesus in the tissue paper. Now let your toddler rub glue on the star. Place the star at the top of the plate. This can be used as a Christmas decoration around the house.

LOW PREP Christmas Tree Counting

Materials:

- ☐ Green Construction Paper
- ☐ Marker
- ☐ Do-a-Dot Markers or Paint

Directions:

Ask your little one if he would like to paint lights on a Christmas tree. Use a marker to draw a Christmas tree on your green construction paper. Now tell your little one you are going to ask him to find a certain color paint and when he finds it you will tell him how many lights to put on the tree in that color. If you are using Do-a-Dot markers, you can ask him to find the color red. When he finds the red Do-a-Dot marker ask him to put one dot on the Christmas tree. Next, ask him to find another color and put two dots on the Christmas tree. Continue until the Christmas tree is full.

If you do not have Do-a-Dot markers, you can use paint and have your little one dip his finger or a q-tip into the paint to make the dots. Ask him to find a color, dip his q-tip in that color, and put the correct number of dots onto the Christmas tree.

LOW PREP Candy Cane Ornaments

Materials:

- ☐ Pipe Cleaners
- ☐ Red and White Pony Beads
- ☐ Scissors

Directions:

Ask your little one if he would like to make candy cane ornaments. Cut about three inches of your pipe cleaner off. Place a bead on the end of the pipe cleaner and fold the end over so that it prevents the beads from sliding off. Now show your little one how to thread the beads onto the pipe cleaner. You can let him design his own candy cane, or you can show him how to make patterns like:

Red, white, red, white

Red, red, white, white, red, red

Red, white, white, red, white, white

White, red, red, white, red, red

When he fills up the pipe cleaner with beads, fold the end of the pipe cleaner over the last bead so the beads don't fall off. Bend the pipe cleaner over so that it looks like a candy cane. You can let your toddler hang it on the Christmas tree as an ornament.

Christmas Tree Squiggly Lines

Materials:

- ☐ Green Construction Paper
- ☐ Marker
- ☐ Paint
- ☐ Paper Plate
- ☐ Q-tips

Directions:

Draw a Christmas tree on a piece of green construction paper. Draw a straight, zigzag, wavy, and dotted line across the tree like they are light strands on the Christmas tree. Add other lines if you would like. Ask your toddler if he would like to paint a Christmas tree.

Show him the Christmas tree you drew. Tell him he can trace the lines with his finger. Next, let him pick a paint color. Squirt some paint onto the paper plate. Tell him he is going to use the q-tip to dip in the paint, and then trace the lines with the q-tip just like he did with his finger.

LOW PREP

Nativity Color by Number

Materials:

- ☐ Nativity Color by Number Activity Page (Appendix AB)
- ☐ Crayons

Directions:

Ask your toddler if he would like to color a picture of Mary, Joseph, and baby Jesus. Show him that the numbers on the page tell him what color to use. Highlight each number with the correct color crayon he is supposed to use. For example, color over the word brown with a brown crayon. Ask your little one what color he is to use in coloring the number "1s". After he answers, ask him to find a number "1" to color. When he finishes with that "1" ask him if he can find any more number "1s" to color. Do this for each number and color.

Insect & Bug Activities

LOW PREP Bug or Not Chart

Materials:

- ☐ Bug or Not Activity Page (Appendix AC)
- ☐ Crayons
- ☐ Scissors
- ☐ Glue

Directions:

Ask your toddler if he wants to learn about bugs and insects. Tell him insects do not have bones like we do. Some bugs have wings. Some bugs have many legs, like six or more.

Show your toddler the *Bug or Not* activity page. Point out some bugs for him to see. Help your toddler cut out the pictures. Hold up a picture and ask him if that picture is a bug or animal. Let him glue it in the correct box. Do this for all the pictures.

LOW PREP Caterpillar Counting

Materials:

- ☐ Caterpillar Counting Activity Page (Appendix AD)
- ☐ Paint or Do-a-Dot Markers

Directions:

Ask your toddler if he would enjoy painting caterpillars. Show him the *Caterpillar Counting* activity page. Tell him that he should look at the number next to the caterpillar's head to know how many body parts to paint on the caterpillar. Point to the number "1", and ask your toddler what number it is. He should answer that it's the number "1." Next your toddler can use a Do-a-Dot marker or dip his finger in paint to put one dot next to the caterpillar's head. Do this for all the caterpillars.

Butterfly Experiment

Materials:

- ☐ Piece of Cardboard
- ☐ Tissue Paper
- ☐ Construction Paper
- ☐ Crayons
- ☐ Scissors
- ☐ Elmer's Glue
- ☐ Balloon

Directions:

Ask your toddler if he wants to make a butterfly flap its wings. Cut out a square of cardboard, about a 7-inch by 7-inch square. Let your toddler assist you in drawing some butterfly wings on the tissue paper. The butterfly wings should be one piece. The butterfly wings need to fit on your square. Cut out the wings. Let your toddler assist you in drawing a butterfly body on the construction paper. The butterfly body needs to be longer than the wings. Cut it out. Place the wings on your cardboard. Do not glue them down. Now place the butterfly body on top of the wings. Use Elmer's glue to glue the butterfly body on top of the wings. The glue will soak through the tissue paper and stick to the cardboard. Let your toddler draw eyes and a mouth on the butterfly.

Blow up a balloon. Let your toddler rub his balloon on the carpet, your hair, or his hair. Ask him to hold the balloon over the butterfly (close but not touching it) and watch the wings raise and lower the closer and further away he gets.

LOW PREP Bug Walk

Materials:

- ☐ Bug Walk Activity Page (Appendix AE)
- ☐ Clipboard
- ☐ Crayons

Directions:

Ask your toddler if he wants to go on a walk and hunt for bugs. Show him the *Bug Walk* activity page. Tell him that on the walk he is going to look for the bugs on the activity page. When he finds them he can color the picture. Let your toddler pick out a crayon, clip the activity page to a clipboard, and enjoy your bug walk.

Ants on a Log Snack

Materials:

- ☐ Celery Sticks
- ☐ Peanut Butter
- ☐ Raisins
- ☐ Knife

Directions:

Ask your toddler if he wants to make a fun bug snack. Tell him that he will make ants on a log. Cut some celery into 4-inch size sticks. Make sure they still have the U-shaped center. Ask your toddler to spread some peanut butter into the U-shaped part of the celery stick. Next, ask him to place some raisins in the peanut butter. Now you have some ants on a log to enjoy!

Left & Right Activities

LOW PREP Yarn Hand

Materials:

- ☐ Yarn
- ☐ Scissors

Directions:

This is an all-day activity. Tie a piece of yarn around your toddler's right wrist. Face your toddler and shake his right hand. Tell him that this is his right hand, and you shake hands using your right hand. Throughout the day ask your toddler to show you his right hand or pick something up with his right hand.

LOW PREP Sticker Hands

Materials:

- ☐ 2 Circle Stickers
- ☐ Marker

Directions:

This is an all-day activity. Tell your toddler he is going to learn his left hand from his right hand. Write a capital "R" on one circle sticker, and write a capital "L" on the other circle sticker. Place the "R" sticker on your toddler's right hand, and tell him it is his right hand. Place the "L" sticker on his left hand, and tell him it is his left hand. Throughout the day ask your toddler to complete certain actions with either hand. For example: "Pick up the car with your left hand," "Turn the page with your right hand," or "Use your left hand to close the door."

LOW PREP Hokey Pokey

Materials:

- ☐ Hokey Pokey Song

Directions:

Ask your toddler if he wants to sing a song and dance. I couldn't quite remember all the words to the Hokey Pokey song so I looked it up on YouTube. Let the song play. Following the instructions given in the lyrics of the song you and your toddler should have a fun time singing and dancing.

LOW PREP Simon Says

Directions:

Ask your toddler if he wants to play a fun game. Tell him it is called "Simon Says" and you will be Simon. You can also call the game "Mommy Says" if the name Simon is too confusing for him. Explain that to play the game you will tell him to do something like "Simon says raise your right hand," and then he should raise his right hand. Explain that if he doesn't hear you say, "Simon says," he is not to do the command. Give your toddler commands such as: "Touch your left foot," "Shake your right hand," or "Stomp your right foot," etc. It is a humorous and fun time, but also a great time of learning.

LOW PREP Color the Picture

Materials:

- ☐ Left and Right Activity Page (Appendix AF)
- ☐ Crayons

Directions:

Ask your toddler if he wants to pick out left and right pictures. Show him the *Left and Right* activity page. Ask him to show you his right hand. Now ask him to show you his left hand. Read the directions from the first box of the activity page to your toddler, and let him color the correct picture. Do this for each box.

Twister

Materials:

- ☐ Construction Paper
- ☐ Scissors
- ☐ Tape or Sticky Tac

Directions:

Pick two different colors of construction paper. Cut out eight medium size circles from each color. Then make a four by four grid on the floor. You will want to do a line of four circles of one color, and then a line of four circles of the other color. I did four red circles in a line about six inches apart, and then a line of four blue circles about six inches from the red circles, and repeated. You want it to look like a twister mat. Tape the circles to the floor.

Ask your toddler if he wants to play Twister. Tell him it's a fun game in which you call out a body part and instruct him where to put it on a colored circle. Give him an example by calling out, "Put your right hand on the red circle." Now place your right hand on a red circle. If needed, after calling out instructions, help guide your toddler in placing the correct body part to the correct colored area on the circle.

Ocean Activities

Jellyfish Bead Counting

Materials:

- ☐ Paper Plate
- ☐ Scissors
- ☐ Marker
- ☐ Single Hole Punch
- ☐ Beads
- ☐ Yarn
- ☐ Tape (optional)

Directions:

Cut a paper plate in half. Pick one of the halves to be your jellyfish. Draw two eyes and a mouth for your jellyfish. Along the straight edge of the plate punch eight to ten holes. Write a number above each hole. Start with the number "1." Cut eight to ten pieces (depending how many holes you punched) of yarn six inches long. Tie one end of the yarn to each hole. Wrap a piece of tape around the other ends of the yarn to keep the yarn from unraveling as your toddler threads the beads.

Ask your toddler if he would like to count beads on a jellyfish. Show him the jellyfish you made. Show him the tentacles that hang down from the jellyfish. Together, count the numbers above the tentacles. Explain to him to look at the number above the tentacle to know how many beads to put on the tentacle. For example, the first tentacle has the number "1" above it so he will thread one bead onto the tentacle.

LOW PREP Writing in Sand

Materials:

- ☐ Pan
- ☐ Sand

Directions:

Ask your toddler if he would like to write and draw in sand. If you have a sandbox, you can do this activity in the sandbox. We don't have a sandbox, so I bought a bag of colored sand from the craft store and poured it in a pencil box. (Now I can do this activity more than once.) After preparing the "sand box," I held up letter flashcards and asked my sons if they could draw the letters. Once they got bored drawing letters we drew shapes and silly pictures.

Feed the Shark

Materials:

- ☐ Large Piece of Cardboard
- ☐ Scissors
- ☐ White Paper
- ☐ Hot Glue Gun
- ☐ Marker
- ☐ Construction Paper

Directions:

You will need to cut a shark head out of your piece of cardboard, and then cut a mouth out of the center. Our shark head looked like the top half of an oval. Our shark mouth looked like an upside down crescent moon. Make your shark teeth by cutting zigzags across the bottom of your white piece of paper. Use the hot glue gun to glue the teeth around the mouth opening. Turn the shark over, and draw some eyes above the mouth. Find a place for it to stand, but make sure there is an opening behind the mouth. I taped mine up against the leg of the kitchen table. Now cut out some fish shapes from construction paper. You can do different colored fish or you can write letters or numbers on the fish.

Ask your toddler if he would like to feed the shark. Place all the fish in front of the shark. You can call out a color, letter or number for your toddler to find and feed to the shark.

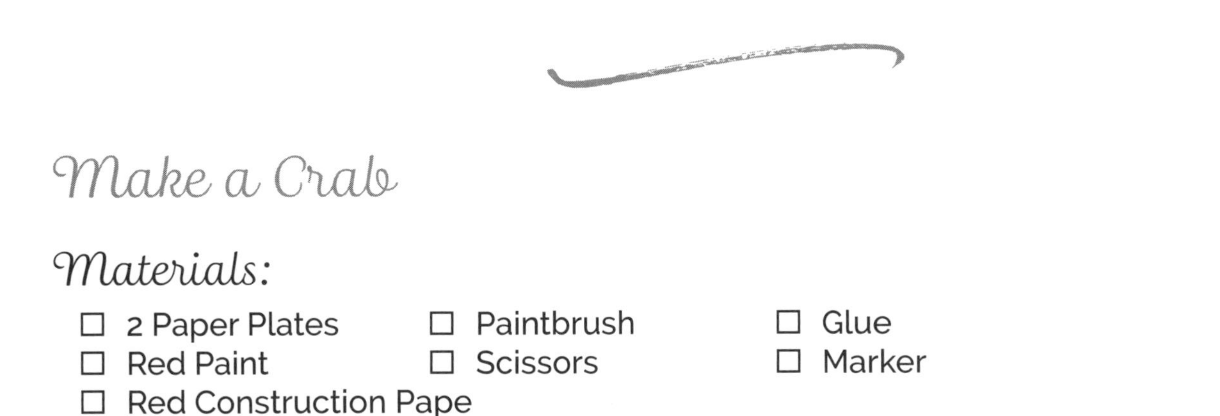

Make a Crab

Materials:

- ☐ 2 Paper Plates
- ☐ Red Paint
- ☐ Red Construction Pape
- ☐ Paintbrush
- ☐ Scissors
- ☐ Glue
- ☐ Marker

Directions:

Ask your toddler if he would like to make a crab. Squirt some red paint on a separate paper plate. Place a paper plate in front of your toddler, and let him paint one side. When he finishes, let the paint dry. After it dries, let him paint the other side red, and let it dry. After both sides are dry, help your toddler fold the paper plate in half. Let your toddler draw a face on the crab. Now turn it over.

Cut eight red strips (one inch wide) from the construction paper. Cut along the width of the paper. Let your toddler glue four strips to the right side of the crab and four strips to the left side of the crab. Flip it back over and you have a cute crab!

Pipe Cleaner Fishing

Materials:

- ☐ Pipe Cleaners
- ☐ Bowl

Directions:

Make a few pipe cleaner fish by holding both ends of the pipe cleaner about three inches from the ends. Bring your fingers together and twist the pipe cleaner together where your fingers meet. Bend the free ends of the pipe cleaner to form a triangle shape, and twist together. To make a fishing hook, take a regular pipe cleaner and bend the end up about an inch to form a hook. Put the fish in a big bowl.

Ask your toddler if he would like to go fishing. Show him the "ocean bowl" full of fish. You can show him how to hook a fish using the pipe cleaner hook, and then let him try.

Salt Water Density Experiment

Materials:

- ☐ Small Plastic Jewels, Grapes, or Eggs
- ☐ 4 Clear Cups
- ☐ Water
- ☐ 2 Tablespoons of Salt
- ☐ 2 Tablespoons of Sugar
- ☐ 2 Tablespoons of Baking Soda
- ☐ Masking Tape
- ☐ Marker
- ☐ Spoon

Directions:

Ask your toddler if he wants to do an experiment to discover how objects float in the ocean. Place a piece of masking tape across each cup. Write salt on one, sugar on one, baking soda on one, and plain on the last piece of masking tape. Let your toddler help you fill each cup with hot water—about 2/3 full. Dissolve 2 tablespoons of salt into the salt cup. Dissolve 2 tablespoons of sugar in the cup labeled sugar. Dissolve 2 tablespoons of baking soda in the cup labeled baking soda. Don't put anything in the plain cup.

Ask your toddler what he thinks will happen when he drops the jewels in each cup of water. Let him drop some jewels into each cup of water to find out if he was right. If the jewels do not float in the baking soda and salt water, you need to add more baking soda and salt to the cups. Explain to your toddler that salt water is heavier than the plain water, so it makes the jewels float.

LOW PREP Where Do We Live?

Materials:

- ☐ Where Do We Live? Activity Page (Appendix AG)
- ☐ Crayons
- ☐ Scissors
- ☐ Glue

Directions:

Ask your toddler if he wants to help you find out what animals live in the ocean. Show him the *Where Do We Live* activity page. Let him color the pictures. Cut out the bottom pictures. If your toddler is good at using scissors, let him help you cut out the pictures. Show your toddler one of the pictures, and ask him if that animal lives in the ocean or on land. Let him glue the animal in the correct spot. Continue this with each picture.

Season Activities

Spring

LOW PREP *Plant Seeds in a Jar*

Materials:

- ☐ Paper Towels
- ☐ Water
- ☐ Seeds
- ☐ Mason Jar

Directions:

Ask your toddler if he would like to plant some seeds to watch them grow. Let your toddler fill the mason jar with paper towels. Let him place the seeds in the paper towels. It's more fun if the seeds are placed close to the glass so your toddler can watch the seed blossom. We planted watermelon seeds, and they did a great job growing! Pour water onto the paper towels. You want the paper towels to be moist, but not soaked or flooded. Let your toddler place the jar in a very sunny spot. Watch the jar each day for any changes. If you notice the paper towels becoming dry, you will need to add some water.

Once our seeds started sprouting and growing roots we transferred the seeds to a mason jar filled with dirt. It was wonderful to watch how they continued to grow. In fact, they grew to the extent we needed to transfer them outside. Unfortunately, I could not think of a way to remove the watermelon plants from the jar so I had to break the jars. So, if you plan to transfer your plants outside, I recommend purchasing little planters to put them in, instead of mason jars.

What is Hiding in the Grass?

Materials:

- ☐ Spring Activity Page (Appendix AH)
- ☐ Green Construction Paper
- ☐ Scissors
- ☐ Glue
- ☐ Toddler Scissors
- ☐ Crayons

Directions:

Cut your green piece of construction paper in strips to look like grass, but only cut the strips all the way down to an inch from the bottom of the page. Now spread glue along that bottom inch of the green construction paper. Lay it along the edge of the *Spring* activity page so it looks like the picture is being hidden by grass.

Ask your toddler if he wants to find out what is hiding in the grass. Tell him he will use his scissors (or his lawnmower) to cut away the grass blades to discover what is hiding in the grass.

Season Activities

Summer

LOW PREP Nature Paintbrushes

Materials:

- ☐ Objects from Nature
- ☐ Paint
- ☐ Paper Plate
- ☐ Paper

Directions:

Ask your toddler if he wants to go on a hunt to find paintbrushes in nature. Take your toddler outside to find different items he can use as a paintbrush. He might select flowers, grass, leaves, tree bark, sticks, or rocks. Once he gathers all his new paintbrushes, go back inside. Then, squirt some paint on a paper plate and let him make a masterpiece using his new paintbrushes.

LOW PREP Make a Solar Oven

Materials:

- ☐ Pizza Box
- ☐ Scissors
- ☐ Page Protector
- ☐ Aluminum Foil
- ☐ Tape
- ☐ Pencil

Directions:

Ask your toddler if he wants to make an oven that works by using heat from the sun. You will need to cut a lid for your oven in the top of the pizza box by cutting a large square, but only cut three sides (one side needs to stay attached for a "hinge"). Make the opening smaller than the page protector. Open the lid. From the inside of your pizza box, tape the page protector onto the top of the pizza box to cover the opening you just made. Tape it securely because this will help trap the heat in the oven. Let your little one help you line the inside of the pizza box with foil. Let your toddler help you wrap a piece of aluminum foil to the inside of the oven lid. You can tape the aluminum foil in place, if needed. Now use a pencil to prop up the new oven lid.

We used our oven to make s'mores since they won't spoil easily. We placed a graham cracker, chocolate, and marshmallow in the oven, and then closed the lid. Place the oven in a sunny spot. Prop the solar panel (oven lid) open facing direct sunlight. Then let your s'more cook. Enjoy!

Fall

Season Activities

LOW PREP

Leaf Color Changing Experiment

Materials:

- ☐ 3 Leaves from the Same Tree
- ☐ Rubbing Alcohol
- ☐ Mason Jar
- ☐ Spoon
- ☐ Plastic Wrap
- ☐ Paper Coffee Filter
- ☐ Small Bowl

Directions:

Ask your toddler if he wants to do an experiment to discover what color leaves will change to in the fall. Explain to him that leaves contain chlorophyll, and chlorophyll is what makes leaves green. Chlorophyll covers up all the other colors in the leaves. To determine what color a leaf would be without chlorophyll you need to separate the colors.

Go outside and let your toddler pick three leaves from the same tree. Let him break the leaves into tiny pieces and put them in the mason jar. Pour rubbing alcohol over the leaves until they are covered completely. Use a spoon to crush and stir the leaves into the rubbing alcohol until the alcohol turns slightly green. Place the plastic wrap tightly over the jar. Place the jar in a small bowl. Pour hot water into the bowl. Let the jar sit in the hot water for at least 30 minutes, occasionally swishing the jar. After 30 minutes, the rubbing alcohol should turn a dark green color.

Cut a strip from the coffee filter, place it in the jar, and let it rest over the side for a little bit. The liquid will travel up the coffee filter. The colors will start to separate as the alcohol evaporates off the coffee filter. Let this process continue for an hour. As the colors separate your toddler should be able to see what color your leaves will become in the fall.

LOW PREP Leaf Rubbings

Materials:

- ☐ Various Leaves
- ☐ Crayons
- ☐ Paper

Directions:

Ask your toddler if he wants to make a leaf picture. Walk outside with him and let him collect different kinds of leaves. Go back inside and let him pick one or two leaves to place under his piece of paper. Next, let him pick a crayon. Show your toddler how to turn the crayon on its side and rub it over the leaf (remember...the leaf is placed under the paper). Your child may want to select other leaves to place under his paper and "rub" over with his crayon.

Winter

Make a Snowflake

Materials:

- ☐ 3 Pipe Cleaners
- ☐ 1/3 Cup of Borax Laundry Soap
- ☐ 2 Cups of Water
- ☐ Scissors
- ☐ String
- ☐ Large Mason Jar
- ☐ Pencil

Directions:

Ask your toddler if he wants to make a snowflake. Cut three pipe cleaners in half. Lay them over each other to look like a snowflake. Twist them together. We kept our snowflake design simple, but you can design your snowflake anyway you want. Now wrap a piece of string around one point of the snowflake securely. Wrap the other end of the string around a pencil. Place the snowflake in the mason jar, and lay the pencil across the opening of the mason jar. The snowflake should be dangling in the mason jar. Pour 2 cups of water in a pot and heat the water until it boils. Add 1/3 cup of Borax and stir until it dissolves. Carefully pour the mixture into the mason jar. Make sure the snowflake is covered with the mixture. You can add another 2 cups of boiling water and 1/3 cup of Borax to the mason jar, if needed. Place the jar somewhere your toddler can watch the snowflake grow. It takes at least 24 hours before crystals form.

LOW PREP Make Play Snow

Materials:

- ☐ ½ Cup of White Conditioner
- ☐ 3 Cups of Baking Soda
- ☐ Bucket

Directions:

Ask your toddler if he wants to make snow and build a snowman! In a bucket mix together your conditioner and baking soda. You can double the recipe if you want more snow. Let your little one squish the snow between his fingers, build a snowman, and use tools to play in it!

All

Tree Paintings

Materials:

- ☐ 4 Pieces of Construction Paper
- ☐ Brown Construction Paper
- ☐ Pencil
- ☐ Scissors
- ☐ Glue
- ☐ Paint
- ☐ Q-tips

Directions:

Ask your toddler if he wants to make trees for each season. Trace his hand and arm four times on a piece of brown construction paper. You might need a couple pieces of brown paper. Cut them out. These will be the tree trunks. Let your toddler pick out four pieces of paper to glue each tree trunk to. Let them glue a tree trunk to each piece of paper.

To make the winter tree, squirt some white paint onto a paper plate, let your toddler dip a q-tip into the paint, and then dot the page with snowflakes falling all over the page. To make the spring tree, you will need green and pink paint. Ask your toddler to dot a few pink flowers on the tree, and then he will need to dot green leaves on the tree. To make the summer tree, your toddler will need to use the q-tip and green paint to fill the tree with green leaf dots. To make the fall tree, your toddler will need to dot the tree with red, yellow, brown, orange, and green leaves. He can even have a few dots on the ground.

LOW PREP What Do You Wear?

Materials:

- ☐ Clothes

Directions:

Ask your toddler if he wants to play dress up. You will call out a season and he will go dress himself in the appropriate clothes for the season. For example, if you said winter, he would put on his coat, mittens, hat, and scarf. He might need some assistance putting certain items on.

LOW PREP

Seasons Sorting

Materials:

- ☐ Seasons Sorting Activity Page (Appendix AI)
- ☐ Scissors
- ☐ Glue

Directions:

Talk to your toddler about the different seasons and some things you might see or do during those seasons. Show your toddler the *Seasons Sorting* activity page. Cut out all the pictures together. Tell your toddler that the first tree shows that it's spring time, the second tree shows summer time, the third tree shows fall time, and the last tree shows winter time. Hold up one of the cut outs and let your toddler decide which season the picture represents. Decide where each picture goes before gluing them down.

LOW PREP

Seasons Sequencing

Materials:

- ☐ Seasons Sequencing Activity Page (Appendix AJ)
- ☐ Scissors
- ☐ Glue

Directions:

Tell your toddler that trees change during each season. Tell them that in the winter trees don't have leaves, but in the spring the leaves start to grow back. By summer the tree is full of leaves, and then in the fall the leaves start to change colors and fall off again. Show him the *Seasons Sequencing* activity page. Cut out the pictures. Ask your toddler if he can remember the first season you mentioned (when the trees are bare and it is really cold outside). Let him glue the winter picture in the first box. Ask him what you said happened after winter. Let him glue the spring picture in the second box. Ask your toddler what you said happened after spring. Let him glue the summer picture in the third box. Ask him what you said happened after summer. Let him glue the fall picture in the last box. Ask your child if he can explain to you what happens to each tree during the seasons.

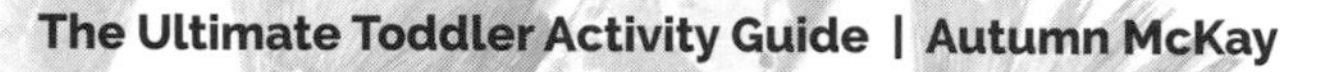

Senses Activities

Seeing

Senses Activities

LOW PREP *Build a Tower Blindfolded*

Materials:

- ☐ Blindfold
- ☐ Blocks

Directions:

Ask your toddler if he wants to build a tower. Tell him he will learn about his five senses: seeing, hearing, smelling, tasting, and touching. Tell him that he sees with his eyes. Tell him he is going to experience what it is like to build a tower when his eyes are covered.

Place the blocks in front of your toddler. Put the blindfold on your toddler. I cut a long strip of cloth from an old t-shirt to use as a blindfold. Ask him to build you a tower.

Missing Items

Materials:

- ☐ Cookie Sheet
- ☐ Various Objects (Ex. Spoon, cars, block, apple, scissors, etc.)

Directions:

Ask your toddler if he wants to play a game. Ask your toddler what body part allows him to see. Place the various items from the materials list on a cookie sheet. Ask your toddler to study the tray to see all the objects—give him about two minutes to study the tray. Ask him to turn around and close his eyes. Remove one object from the tray and hide it. Ask your toddler to turn back around. Ask him if he can tell you which object is missing from the tray. Continue to remove the items (each time asking if your little one can name the missing item) until all the objects are gone. My sons wanted to play this game again and again. They also enjoyed adding more objects to the tray.

LOW PREP Blindfold Drawing

Materials:

- ☐ Blindfold
- ☐ Paper
- ☐ Crayons

Directions:

Ask your toddler if he can draw you a picture of different shapes, a picture of himself, or a picture of something he really enjoys drawing. After he finishes drawing his picture, tell him it would be fun to see if he could draw the same picture while he is blindfolded.

Place the blindfold on your toddler. Let him try to draw the same picture. When he finishes, take the blindfold off and let him compare the two pictures. Ask him what we use to see with. Ask him why he thinks the second picture was not as good as the first picture.

Hearing

Mystery Sound Eggs

Materials:

- ☐ 10 Plastic Eggs
- ☐ Dried Beans
- ☐ Coins
- ☐ Marbles
- ☐ Corn Kernels
- ☐ Rice
- ☐ Tape

Directions:

From your materials list, fill two plastic eggs with the same material (dried beans, coins, marbles, corn kernels or rice). Of your ten eggs, you will create five sets of eggs having the same materials (two eggs filled with dried beans, two eggs filled with coins, two eggs filled with marbles etc.) Tape the eggs shut to prevent any messes. Place the ten eggs in a box or basket.

Ask your toddler if he wants to play a sound matching game. Tell your toddler that we use our ears to hear, so today he will play a hearing game. Hand your toddler the basket containing the ten eggs. Tell him to select an egg, shake it, and listen to the sound it makes. Now, he should shake the other eggs in the basket, attempting to find the egg making the same sound when shaken. After your toddler has matched each egg, open the eggs up to see if he matched them correctly.

LOW PREP Water Xylophone

Materials:

- ☐ Glasses and/or Vases
- ☐ Water

Directions:

Ask your toddler if he would like to make a xylophone. Ask him what body part he uses to hear sounds. Select several glasses or vases. I used six drinking glasses. Ask your toddler to help you fill the glasses. Fill the glasses to various levels so that no two are alike. Let your toddler tap on the glasses with his finger or the end of a metal spoon. We used our fingers at first so I could judge how hard they would tap. Line the glasses along a table in order from greatest amount of water to least amount of water. Encourage your toddler to create a song by tapping on the glasses.

LOW PREP

Guess What I'm Doing

Materials:

- ☐ Blindfold

Directions:

Ask your toddler what he uses his ears to do. Tell him he is going to use his ears today to try to guess what Mommy is doing. Tell him he will be blindfolded and you will do something, like close a door and he will have to guess what Mommy just did.

Place the blindfold on your toddler. Do the activity you used as an example, and ask your toddler if he knew what you did by the sounds he heard. If needed, you can give him hints until he clearly understands the game. Examples of actions to try are: close a door, push keys on a keyboard, jingle car keys, fill a cup with water, bounce a ball, zip a coat, etc. Now let your toddler make a sound while you are blindfolded.

Smelling

Senses Activities

Spice Painting

Materials:

- ☐ 5 Different Spices
- ☐ 5 Bowls
- ☐ 5 Paintbrushes
- ☐ Paper

Directions:

Pick out five spices that have strong scents. If unsure, try using cinnamon, celery salt, garlic powder, onion powder, and sage. Fill five small bowls with your spices, one spice per bowl, and add some water. Stir each mixture together. These five bowls will be your toddler's paint buckets.

Ask your toddler if he wants to paint a smelly picture. Tell him that smelling is one of our senses, and we use our nose to smell things. Let him smell each bowl of paint. Ask him which one he liked smelling. Place a paintbrush in each bowl and ask your toddler to paint a picture using the smelly paints. Let the picture dry. Let your toddler smell the picture to see how it smells.

LOW PREP Make Scented Playdough

Materials:

- ☐ 1 Cup of Flour
- ☐ ¼ Cup of Salt
- ☐ 2 Tablespoons of Cream of Tartar
- ☐ 1 Pack of Unsweetened Kool-Aid
- ☐ 1 Cup of Water
- ☐ 1 Tablespoon of Vegetable Oil
- ☐ Pot
- ☐ Spoon

Directions:

Ask your toddler what body part he uses for smelling. Ask him if he would like to make some smelly playdough. Let your toddler pour flour, salt, cream of tartar, and Kool-Aid in a medium pot. Stir in the oil. Mix the ingredients together over medium heat for three to five minutes until it starts to form a ball. Remove it from the pan. Be careful. It will be hot! Knead the dough until soft and cool. Let your toddler play in the playdough with letters, cookie cutters, or utensils. When he is finished store the playdough in an airtight container or bag—it will help provide many more days of fun.

LOW PREP

Identify Family Members by Smell

Materials:

- ☐ A Worn Shirt from Each Family Member
- ☐ Blindfold

Directions:

Ask your toddler if he wants to use his nose to play a game. Tell him you will cover his eyes with a blindfold and hand him a shirt. Ask him to smell the shirt and guess which family member it belongs to. Clothes recently worn may work a little better than clothes from the laundry room.

Tasting

Taste Test

Materials:

- ☐ A Food for Sweet, Sour, Salty, Spicy, and Bitter
- ☐ Muffin Tin

Directions:

Tell your toddler that tongues help us taste foods. Taste is one of our five senses. Ask him if he would like to have a taste test to try some different flavors of food. You can blindfold your toddler if you would like, and ask him to guess what he ate, or just give him new foods to try that he has never tasted.

I chose to blindfold my sons because they are picky eaters and probably would not try new foods. I put a food from each category in a muffin tin. I chose a strawberry for the sweet item, a pickle for the sour item, a pretzel for the salty item, salsa for the spicy item, and semi-sweet chocolate chips for the bitter item. Hand your toddler a piece of food to try. Ask him what it tastes like, if he likes it, and if he can guess what he is eating. It's fun to hear the guesses!

LOW PREP Jelly Bean Taste Experiment

Materials:

- ☐ Bag of Jelly Beans

Directions:

Ask your toddler what body part is used to taste things. Tell him to close his eyes, and you will hand him a jelly bean. Ask him to eat the jelly bean and try to guess its flavor and color. My sons especially enjoyed the Starburst jelly beans.

LOW PREP

Make Cookies Together and Eat Them

Materials:

- ☐ Cookie Ingredients
- ☐ 1 Cup of All-Purpose Flour
- ☐ 1 Teaspoon of Baking Soda
- ☐ ¼ Teaspoon of Salt
- ☐ 1 Stick of Unsalted Butter
- ☐ ½ Cup of Creamy Peanut Butter
- ☐ 1/3 Cup of Brown Sugar
- ☐ ½ Cup of Granulated Sugar
- ☐ ½ Teaspoon of Vanilla Extract
- ☐ 1 Egg
- ☐ ½ Cup of Oats
- ☐ 1 Cup of Semisweet Chocolate Chips
- ☐ 2 Bowls
- ☐ Cookie Sheet
- ☐ Spoon

Directions:

Ask your toddler if he wants to make cookies today and taste them. It's fun if you try a new recipe so he can taste the new flavors. Our favorite cookie recipe is a chocolate chip peanut butter oatmeal cookie—it has everything!

To make these cookies you will need to preheat the oven to 350 degrees Fahrenheit. Ask your toddler to whisk together the flour, baking soda, and salt in a small bowl, and set aside. I used my Kitchen Aid mixer for this next part. Ask your toddler to pour the butter, peanut butter, sugar, brown sugar and vanilla into the mixing bowl. Cream those ingredients together on medium speed for about three minutes. Add the egg and beat that until it is combined. Now ask your toddler to scoop in the flour mixture and start to mix it together on low speed. Stir in the oats and chocolate chips by hand.

Scoop a 1 to 2-inch sized ball onto a cookie sheet. Make them two inches apart. Bake the cookies for 10 minutes, or until lightly golden. Place them on a cooling rack to cool before enjoying them with your toddler.

Touch

Senses Activities

Feel Bags

Materials:

- ☐ 5-10 Brown Lunch Bags
- ☐ 5-10 Objects that Fit in the Bags

Directions:

While your toddler is busy playing, fill each brown bag with an object from the house. Try to find objects with different textures. You can fill the bags with cotton balls, a crayon, craft stick, wash cloth, apple, rubber band, etc. Each bag should only have one object.

Tell your toddler that we use our fingers to touch and feel things. This is one of our five senses. Line your brown bags up in front of your toddler. Tell him you put something in each bag. Ask him to close his eyes and stick his hand in the bag to feel the object. As he is feeling the object ask him to describe what the object feels like. At first, you might have to help him with some words to describe an object. Ask your little one if he knows what is in the bag. After he guesses, pull out the object to see if he was right. After my sons played this game they wanted to fill the bags themselves and make me guess.

Homemade Finger Paint

Materials:

- ☐ 4 Tablespoons of Cornstarch
- ☐ Cold Water
- ☐ 1 Cup of Boiling Water
- ☐ Bowls
- ☐ Whisk
- ☐ Pot
- ☐ Spoon
- ☐ Variety of Food Coloring

Directions:

Ask your toddler if he wants to help you make finger paint. In a bowl mix together the cornstarch and some cold water. You want just enough to make a paste. Make sure there are no lumps. Pour one cup boiling water into the paste mixture and continue to whisk until smooth. Place the mixture in the pot and turn the stove on low heat until you see clear streaks in the mixture. Turn the stove off and continue to stir with a spoon until it gets thick and gooey. Divide your paint into small bowls. Let your toddler add food coloring to each bowl and stir until combined.

Ask your toddler what body part he uses to touch and feel. Explain that he will be able to use the paint he made and his fingers as paintbrushes, to paint a fun picture of his choosing. When he finishes his masterpiece, hang it on the refrigerator.

LOW PREP Touch Scavenger Hunt

Directions:

Ask your toddler how he uses his fingers. Ask him if he would like to go on a touch scavenger hunt. This can be an indoor or outdoor scavenger hunt. Ask him to find items that feel hard, soft, smooth, rough, squishy, prickly, wet and cold. It's fun if you both find items in each category!

All

LOW PREP Popcorn Fun

Materials:

- ☐ Popcorn

Directions:

Pop a bag of popcorn. Ask your toddler if he wants to use all five of his senses to describe the popcorn. Ask your toddler if he can name the five senses. Ask your toddler to use his eyes to see what the popcorn looks like, and ask him to tell you (white, yellow, bumpy, etc.). You might have to ask him some questions to help prompt him to describe the popcorn. Now ask your toddler to hold a piece of popcorn and tell you what it feels like (soft, warm, etc.). Ask your toddler to smell the popcorn and tell you what it smells like (yummy, buttery, etc.). Ask your toddler to eat a piece of popcorn and tell you what it sounds like (crunchy, loud, etc.). Ask your toddler to eat another piece of popcorn and tell you what it tastes like (yummy, buttery, salty, etc.). Now you and your toddler can enjoy the rest of the popcorn together!

LOW PREP Five Senses Matching

Materials:

- ☐ Five Senses Matching Activity Page (Appendix AK)
- ☐ Crayons

Directions:

Ask your toddler if he wants to match the five senses. Show him the *Five Senses Matching* activity page. Point to each body part on the left side and ask what he uses each body part for. Point to the cookie picture and ask your toddler what he does with a cookie. He will probably say, "Eat it!" Ask him what body part he uses to taste or eat things. After he answers, ask him to draw a line from the cookie to the mouth. Do this for each picture.

Shape Activities

Chalk Shape Jump

Materials:

- ☐ Chalk

Directions:

Draw some shapes on the sidewalk. I drew shapes like circle, square, heart, triangle, rectangle, and star. You could also add diamond, crescent, and oval shapes if your toddler is familiar with those shapes. Go through and tell your toddler what each shape is called. Tell him you will call out a shape and he must jump to the correct shape. You can play this game until he is tired—which might be a long time!

LOW PREP Shape Tracing

Materials:

- ☐ Shape Tracing Activity Page (Appendix AL)
- ☐ Crayons, Stickers, Do-a-Dot Markers

Directions:

Show your toddler the *Shape Tracing* activity page. Review each shape with your toddler. Ask him if he would like to draw the shapes with a crayon, put stickers around the shape lines, or use the Do-a-Dot markers to trace the shapes. Let him use whichever method he chooses to trace each shape. You might have to help guide his hand in the beginning if he chooses to trace with crayons.

Shape Erasing

Materials:

- ☐ Chalk
- ☐ Cup of Water
- ☐ Paintbrush

Directions:

Draw some shapes on the sidewalk with chalk. Explain to your toddler that he will dip the paintbrush in the water and trace over the chalk lines to try to erase the shape. Before he starts erasing the shape, ask him what shape he is attempting to erase. My sons thought it was quite fun to be able to erase my shapes, but little did they know they were working on their prewriting skills and shape recognition.

Shape Puzzles

Materials:

- ☐ 8 Paper Plates
- ☐ Marker
- ☐ Crayons
- ☐ Scissors

Directions:

On each paper plate you will draw a big shape right in the middle of the plate. Draw a circle, square, heart, triangle, star, diamond, rectangle, and oval. Color in each shape with a different color. Now cut each paper plate into three or four pieces.

Ask your toddler if he would like to do some puzzles. Explain that he needs to put the pieces back together to form the correct shapes. Spread out all of the pieces in front of your toddler. It's best to focus on one shape at a time. If your little one is struggling, you can tell him to find all the same colored pieces to be able to put a shape together.

LOW PREP

Shape Sorting Hunt

Materials:

- ☐ 3 Paper Lunch Bags
- ☐ Marker

Directions:

Ask your toddler if he wants to go on a shape hunt. On the outside of each lunch bag draw a square, a circle, and a triangle. Ask your toddler to grab the circle bag and walk around the house collecting any circles he sees and put them in his bag. After he fills up his circle bag ask him to fill up his square and triangle bags.

Now you can pour each bag out into one big pile, mix up the items, and ask your toddler to put the items in the correct "shape bag." If your toddler had enough fun after searching for the shapes, you can save the second part of this activity for another time.

Space Activities

LOW PREP

Moon Paintings

Materials:

- ☐ Black Construction Paper
- ☐ White Crayon
- ☐ White Paint
- ☐ Paper Plate
- ☐ Paintbrush
- ☐ Water Bottle Lid

Directions:

Ask your toddler what are some objects he might see in space or at night. Listen to his answer. Ask him if he wants to paint the moon. Use a white crayon to draw a big circle on the black construction paper. Squirt some white paint on a paper plate. Hand your little one a paintbrush. Ask him to paint the moon white. You might have to explain to him that the moon is just inside the circle.

When he finishes painting, and the paint is still wet, explain to your toddler that the moon has craters on it. You can tell him craters are big holes in the moon from where space rocks have hit the moon. Ask your toddler if he wants to add some craters to his moon. Hand him an empty water bottle with the lid on and let him stamp his moon with the water bottle lid.

LOW PREP

Sticker Constellations

Materials:

- ☐ Black Construction Paper
- ☐ White Crayon
- ☐ Star Stickers

Directions:

Tell your little one that there are a lot of stars in the sky and sometimes you can see a big group of stars that make a picture. Tell him this group of stars is called a constellation. You can show him pictures of some constellations. Ask him if he would like to make constellations. You can let your toddler place star stickers anywhere on his black paper. When he finishes, ask him to connect the stickers using the white crayon to form a picture.

For my sons, I lined up the star stickers in the Big Dipper formation and helped them connect the stars to be the Big Dipper. I told them what constellation it was, and explained that it looked like a ladle. Then I let them make their own constellations.

LOW PREP Planets Orbiting the Sun

Materials:

- ☐ Pie Pan
- ☐ Yellow Playdough
- ☐ Small Ball

Directions:

Tell your toddler that there are eight planets in space that spin around the sun. Tell him that when the planets spin around the sun this is called an orbit. Ask him if he wants you to demonstrate how planets orbit the sun. Get a small ball of yellow playdough and flatten the playdough in the center of your pie pan. Explain to your toddler that the yellow playdough is the sun. Now place a small ball (I used a bouncy ball) on the inside edge of your pie pan. Explain that the ball is a planet. Now turn the pie pan so the ball spins around the sun. Let your toddler try to make the planet orbit the sun. You may need to assist your toddler.

Marble Paint Planets

Materials:

- ☐ White Construction Paper
- ☐ Tape
- ☐ Scissors
- ☐ Box
- ☐ Marbles
- ☐ Paint
- ☐ Glue

Directions:

Cut out some circles of different sizes to represent planets. You can cut out as many as you would like. Place the planets in the bottom of a box. Tape them down so they do not move.

Ask your toddler if he wants to use marbles to paint some planets. Dip a few marbles in different colored paint. Place the marbles on top of each circle. Now for the fun part, tell your toddler to shake the box so the marbles move around. If you have a two year old like mine, you might want to close the top of the box until your toddler is finished shaking, and let the painting be a surprise.

When your toddler is finished shaking the box, take the planets out of the box to dry. Once they are dry, let your toddler glue them onto a black piece of construction paper to make a space scene. Let him add a few star stickers, as well.

Star Number Hunt

Materials:

- ☐ Star Number Hunt Activity Page (Appendix AM)
- ☐ Scissors
- ☐ Crayons

Directions:

Cut out the ten stars from the *Star Number Hunt* activity page. While your toddler is busy playing, hide the ten stars around the house.

Ask your toddler if he would like to hunt for some stars. Tell him there are ten stars hidden around the house and when he finds one he needs to bring it back to you. Ask him to say the number that is on the star. Find the number on the activity page and color it. After he colors the number, he can go search for another star.

Rocket Kabobs

Materials:

- ☐ Skewers
- ☐ Strawberries
- ☐ Bananas
- ☐ Kiwi
- ☐ Cantaloupe
- ☐ Knife

Directions:

You will need to prepare the fruit by slicing the bananas into 2-inch chunks. Slice the kiwis. Cut the tops off the strawberries. Cut the cantaloupe into triangle shapes.

Ask your toddler if he would like to make a rocket snack. While you are making your rockets talk about how we use rockets to fly to space and explore the planets. Tell them that people called astronauts ride on the rockets. Instruct your little one to slide a cantaloupe piece to the end of his skewer—the small side of the triangle should be pointing up. This is the tail of the rocket. Now slide a banana chunk down on top of the cantaloupe. Slide a kiwi on top of the banana. Slide another banana on top of the kiwi. Finish the rocket off by placing a strawberry on top of the end of the skewer. Make as many rockets as you would like and enjoy your snack!

Rocket Name

Materials:

- ☐ Construction Paper
- ☐ Scissors
- ☐ Marker
- ☐ Glue

Directions:

Cut several 2-inch by 2-inch squares out of construction paper. They can all be the same color or different colors. You need one square for each letter in your toddler's name. You will need to cut out a triangle for the top of the rocket and two triangle wings for the bottom of the rocket. You can cut out some flames for the bottom of the rocket, as well. Now write one letter from your toddler's name on each square. Make sure the letters are all uppercase.

Ask your toddler if he wants to spell his name and build a rocket at the same time. Show him each square has a letter from his name. If he has never spelled his name before, write it out on a piece of paper for him to see it. You can point and say each letter together. Ask him to put the letters in order to spell his name. Place a piece of construction paper in front of him. Have him glue the rocket top to the top of the paper. Ask your toddler to glue the first letter of his name underneath the triangle piece. Next, he can glue the second letter underneath the first and so on until he gets to the end of his name. Ask your toddler to glue a wing on each side of the last letter of his name. Ask him to glue the flames underneath the last letter of his name. Point to each letter in his name, say the letter together, and then say his name.

Spanish Activities

If you are unfamiliar with Spanish please lookup the correct pronunciation of the Spanish words being taught in these lessons.

Spanish Colors

Red-rojo
Blue-azul
Yellow-amarillo
Green-verde
Orange-anaranjado
Purple-violeta
Pink-rosa
Brown-marron
Black-negro
White-blanco

LOW PREP *Cereal Sort*

Materials:

- ☐ Paper
- ☐ Crayons
- ☐ Fruit Loops

Directions:

Ask your toddler if he would like to learn some colors in Spanish. On a piece of paper draw six circles. Draw one red circle, and color it in. Tell your toddler that circle is rojo; rojo means red. Draw one blue circle, and color it in. Tell your toddler that circle is azul; azul means blue. Draw one yellow circle, and color it in. Tell your toddler that circle is amarillo; amarillo means yellow. Draw one green circle, and color it in. Tell your toddler that circle is verde; verde means green. Draw one orange circle, and color it in. Tell your toddler that circle is anaranjado; anaranjado means orange. Draw one purple circle, and color it in. Tell your toddler that circle is violeta; violeta means purple.

Now explain to your toddler that he is going to match the colored fruit loops to the correct colored circle. When he picks up a fruit loop ask him what color it is. He will probably tell you the color in English. If so, ask him if he knows the Spanish word for that color. Now ask him to place the fruit loop on the correct circle.

Hidden Colors

Materials:

- ☐ Muffin Tin
- ☐ Food Coloring
- ☐ Baking Soda
- ☐ Vinegar
- ☐ Squirt Bottle

Directions:

In a muffin tin place one drop of food coloring in the bottom of each cup. If you only have the standard set of food coloring (red, blue, yellow, and green) you can mix the colors to make different colors. For example, put a drop of yellow and red in one cup to make orange. Now place ½ a teaspoon of baking soda over each drop of food coloring. Pour some vinegar into a squirt bottle—the condiment squirt bottles work great.

Ask your toddler if he wants to do a fun experiment to find colors in Spanish. Ask your toddler to squirt some vinegar onto one muffin cup and see what happens. It's so fun to watch the expressions on a toddler's face as the color appears and starts to fizz! Ask him what color it is. He will probably tell you in English so ask him if he can tell you the answer in Spanish.

Spanish Body Parts

Head-la cabeza
Eyes-los ojos
Ears-las orejas
Nose-la nariz
Mouth-la boca
Shoulder-el hombre
Arm-el brazo
Hand-la mano
Fingers-los dedos
Leg-la pierna
Foot-el pie
Toes-dedos del pie

LOW PREP *Chalk Body*

Materials:

- ☐ Chalk

Directions:

Ask your toddler if he wants to learn parts of the body in Spanish. Go outside and ask your toddler to lie on the driveway. Trace an outline of your toddler with the chalk. Let your little one stand up and decorate the body. Ask him to draw eyes, nose, mouth, hair, clothes, shoes, etc. When he is finished ask him to point to the head. Tell him the Spanish name for head. Ask him to say, "La cabeza." You can continue to ask him to find different parts of the body and tell him the Spanish name. Each time, ask him to repeat the word after you have pronounced it.

Spanish Clothes

Pants-los pantalones
Shirt-la camisa
Dress-el vestido
Coat-el abrigo
Gloves-los guantes
Scarf-la bufanda
Hat-la gorra
Shoes-los zapatos
Boots-las botas
Pajamas-el pijama

Dress a Bear

Materials:

- ☐ Dress a Bear Activity Page (Appendix AN)
- ☐ Crayons
- ☐ Scissors

Directions:

Ask your toddler if he wants to learn the names of different clothes in Spanish. Show him the *Dress a Bear* activity page. Tell him that he is going to dress a bear. Let your toddler color the clothes if he would like. Cut out each piece of clothing. Hold up each piece of clothing for your toddler and say the name of it in Spanish. Ask your toddler to repeat it. Let your toddler dress the bear. As he is dressing the bear ask him to tell you the Spanish word for the clothes he is putting on the bear.

Spanish Numbers

Spanish Activities

1-uno
2-dos
3-tres
4-cuatro
5-cinco
6-seis
7-siete
8-ocho
9-nueve
10-diez

LOW PREP *Snack Counting*

Materials:

- ☐ Toddler's Favorite Snack
- ☐ 10 Index Cards
- ☐ Marker

Directions:

Ask your toddler if he wants to learn numbers in Spanish. Write the numbers 1-10 on index cards—one number for each card. Line the cards up, in numerical order, in front of your toddler. Point to each card and say the number in Spanish. Ask your toddler to repeat.

Let your toddler pick out his favorite snack. My sons' favorite snacks are goldfish and fruit snacks. Tell your toddler he is going to place the correct number of snack items on each card. For example, when he gets to the "5" card; ask him the Spanish word for five. Next, together with your toddler, count out five snack items in Spanish as your little one places each one on the card.

Spelling Name Activities

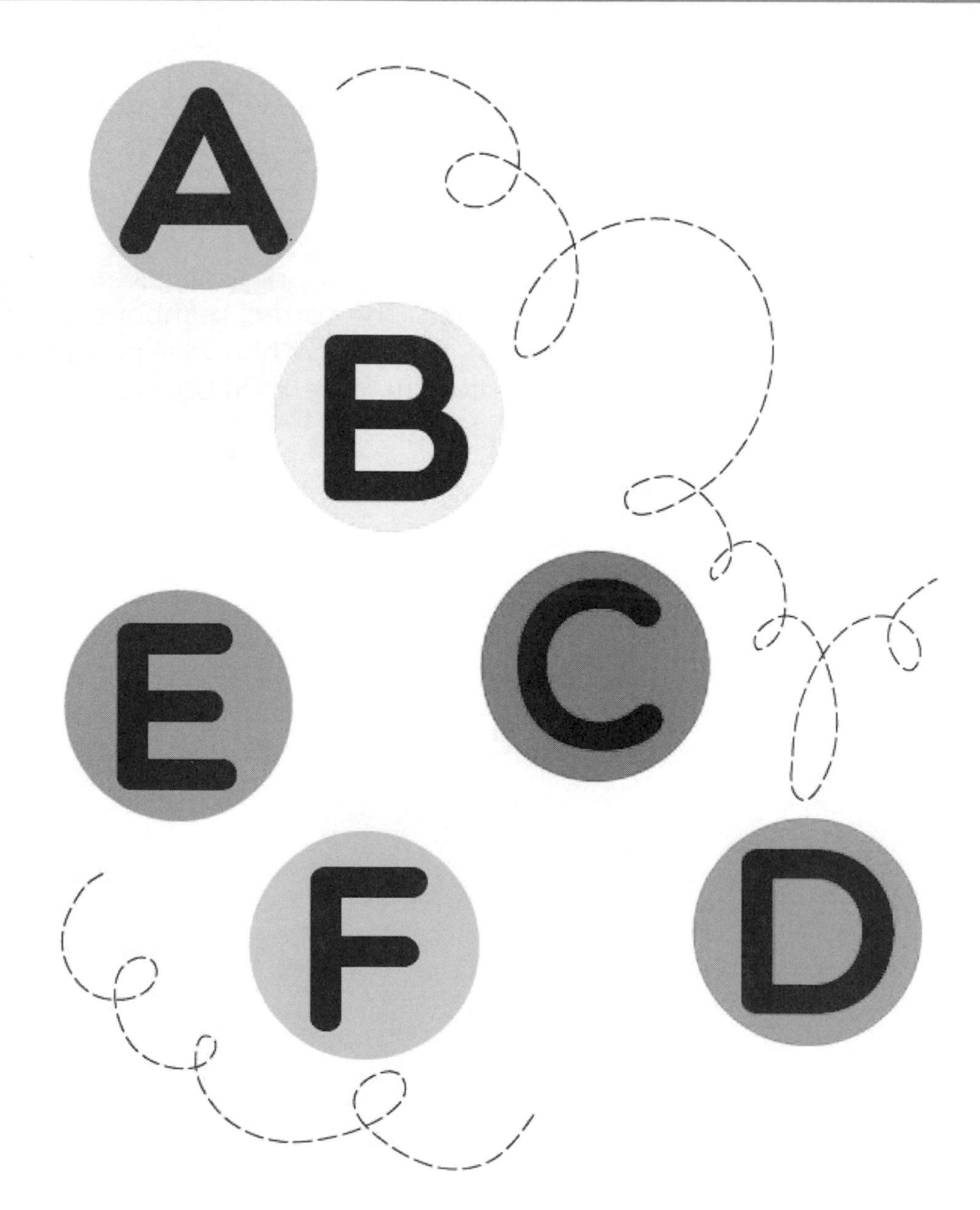

LOW PREP Playdough Imprint Name

Materials:

- ☐ Playdough
- ☐ Magnet Letters or Pom Poms

Directions:

Ask your toddler if he wants to play with playdough. Get out some playdough and flatten it out. Now place the magnet letters from your little one's name in front of him. Ask him to take the first letter of his name, say it, and then press it into the playdough. Do the same with all the letters from his name. When he finishes, have him say each letter as you point to it, and then say his name at the end as your finger scrolls across the bottom of his name. It helps him learn his name if you can sing the spelling of his name in a song.

If you don't have magnet letters you can still do this activity using a pencil and pom poms. Flatten the playdough out. Use a pencil to write the letters of your toddler's name into the playdough. Write in all uppercase letters. Next, have your toddler place pom poms over the pencil lines. Follow the steps about saying each letter and reading the name.

Name Hunt

Materials:

- ☐ Rice
- ☐ Bucket
- ☐ Magnet Letters
- ☐ Paper
- ☐ Marker

Directions:

Ask your toddler if he wants to go on a hunt for his name. Pour a bag of rice into a bucket. (I bought a cheap five pound bag from the grocery store.) Gather the letters from your toddler's name from your magnet letters. Hide them in the bucket of rice. Write your toddler's name on a piece of paper in all uppercase letters. Ask your toddler to help you spell his name. Say each letter together with your toddler as you point to the letter. Next, scroll your finger across the bottom of his name and say his name.

Tell your toddler he will need to dig in the rice to find each letter of his name. When he finds a letter have him place it on top of the letter on his paper. After he finds all his letters you can help him spell his name again.

Name Lego Tower

Materials:

- ☐ Big Legos or Mega Blocks
- ☐ Painter's Tape
- ☐ Marker

Directions:

Ask your toddler if he wants to build his name with Legos. Gather together the same number of Legos as in your toddler's name. Place a piece of painter's tape on the side of each Lego. With a marker write a letter from his name on each Lego. Make sure each letter is uppercase. Place all the letters in front of your toddler in random order. Ask your toddler what letter comes first in his name. Let him find it. Ask him what comes next. Let him find it, and place it underneath the first letter. Continue until he spells his name. After he spells his name, point to each letter and together with him say the name of the letter. Say his whole name as you swipe your finger down the tower. If he is having trouble finding a letter, tell him the letter to look for or write his name on a piece of paper as a guide.

Spell Name with Cars

Materials:

- ☐ Toy Cars
- ☐ Circle Labeling Stickers
- ☐ Post-It Notes
- ☐ Marker
- ☐ Masking or Painter's Tape

Directions:

Ask your toddler if he would like to park cars. Tell him he is going to spell his name with cars. All you need to do is write out the letters (in uppercase) from your toddler's name on Post-it notes. There should be one letter on each Post-it note. Place the Post-it notes in order, along the floor in a straight line. I placed them at the edge of the fireplace. Place a piece of tape between each letter to make it look like parking spots for the cars. Next you will need to write the same letters on the circle labeling stickers. There should be one letter for each sticker. You can place one label on each car. Now explain to your toddler that he will drive the cars and park them in the parking spot with the matching letter. Show him an example. After he parks all the cars, say the letters together and then swipe your finger underneath his name as you say his name.

LOW PREP *Name Puzzle*

Materials:

- ☐ Paper
- ☐ Marker
- ☐ Scissors

Directions:

Write your toddler's name on a piece of paper in uppercase letters. Cut it apart so that each letter is its own puzzle piece. Ask your toddler if he would like to do a puzzle. Lay all the puzzle pieces in front of him in random order. Tell him that the puzzle is his name. See if he can put it together. If he is struggling or if you believe this would be difficult for your toddler, you can write his name on a piece of paper and set it in front of him to use as a guide. When he completes the puzzle, point to each letter in his name and say it together. Read his name as you swipe your finger underneath.

LOW PREP *Pop That Name*

Materials:

- ☐ Bubble Wrap
- ☐ Marker

Directions:

Ask your toddler if he wants to "pop" the letters of his name. Write his name, in uppercase letters, across bubble wrap. Explain to him that he will pop the bubbles as he traces each letter of his name. When he finishes popping the bubbles, point to each letter in his name and say it together. Now read his name as you swipe your finger underneath.

Transportation Activities

Land

Car Graphing

Materials:

- ☐ Poster Board
- ☐ Crayons
- ☐ Marker
- ☐ Toy Cars

Directions:

Make a color graph. On a poster board draw nine lines down the poster to make ten columns. At the bottom of each column draw a colored square. You will need a white, red, orange, yellow, green, blue, purple, brown, gray, and black square.

Ask your toddler if he wants to sort cars to see which color he has the most of. Tell him he is learning about transportation this week. Transportation involves things that go. This week he will do activities with things that go on land like cars, trains, bicycles, etc. Tell him he will pick out a toy car, decide what color it is, and then park it in the correct color column. After he graphs as many cars as he wants, ask him which color he has the most and least of. My sons did this activity many days.

LOW PREP Car Paint and Wash

Materials:

- ☐ Toy Cars
- ☐ Paint
- ☐ Paper Plate
- ☐ Paper
- ☐ Bucket of Water
- ☐ Dish Soap
- ☐ Toothbrush

Directions:

Ask your toddler to pick five of his favorite toy cars. Squirt some paint on a paper plate, and place a piece of paper in front of him. Tell your toddler that his toy cars can go roll in the mud so it will make tracks across the paper. Show him that it's ok to roll his car in the paint, and then roll it across the paper. Let him make some cool designs on his paper.

When he finishes his painting, tell your little one that it's time to take the cars to the car wash. Squirt some dish soap in a bucket of water and let your toddler use a toothbrush to clean his cars.

LOW PREP Make Traffic Lights

Materials:

- ☐ Graham Crackers
- ☐ Nutella or Chocolate Icing
- ☐ Red, Green, and Yellow M&Ms
- ☐ Knife

Directions:

Ask your toddler if he wants to make traffic light snacks. Break apart the graham cracker along the perforated edges. You will use the rectangle piece. Ask your toddler to use a knife to spread Nutella or chocolate icing across the graham cracker. Let your toddler place a red M&M at the top of the rectangle. Next, let him place a yellow M&M underneath the red one. Lastly, he can place a green M&M underneath the yellow one. Enjoy your traffic light snack!

LOW PREP How Far Does It Go?

Materials:

- ☐ Toy Cars
- ☐ Slide or Ramp
- ☐ Tape Measure

Directions:

Ask your toddler if he wants to measure how far cars go. Pull a tape measure out about 20 inches, lock it, and place it at the bottom of the slide. Ask your toddler to pick out a car. Ask him to roll the car down the slide. Come around to the tape measure to show your toddler the distance the car rolled. You can leave the car there and let your toddler roll another car down the slide. Ask your toddler if the second car rolled farther than the first one. Come around to the tape measure and show him the distance the second car rolled. You can keep doing this as long as your little one wants.

Air

LOW PREP Fly Paper Airplanes

Materials:

- ☐ Paper

Directions:

Ask your toddler if he would like to fly paper airplanes. Tell him another way people travel is by flying in the air on an airplane, helicopter, rocket, or hot air balloon. You can fold an airplane for him or let him copy you as you fold one. Show him how to hold and throw the airplane so it will glide through the air. You can have a competition to see whose airplane flies the farthest.

Helicopter Craft

Materials:

- ☐ Construction Paper
- ☐ Craft Sticks
- ☐ Scissors
- ☐ Glue
- ☐ Cotton Balls
- ☐ Crayons

Directions:

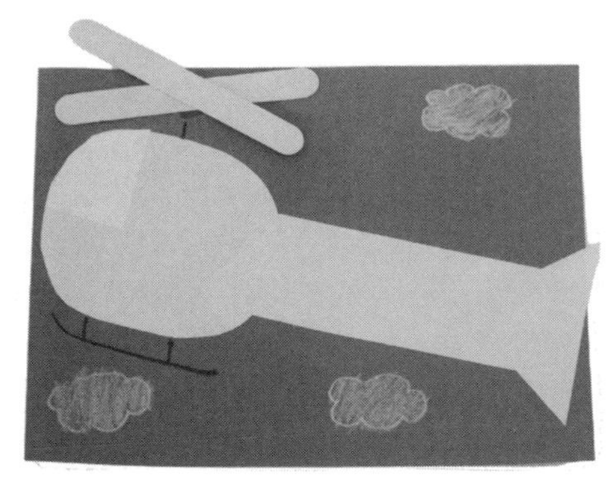

Ask your toddler if he wants to make a helicopter. Let him pick a piece of paper for his helicopter. Cut out an oval shape for the cab of the helicopter. Cut out a rectangle from the same piece of paper for the tail of the helicopter. Cut out a triangle from the same piece of paper for the propeller of the helicopter. Cut out a quarter circle from a white piece of construction paper that will fit on the oval to be the window of the helicopter.

Place a blue piece of construction paper in front of your toddler. This is the sky he will glue his helicopter to. Ask your toddler to rub glue all over the oval. Ask him to place the oval on the left side of his paper and press it down. Ask him to rub glue on the rectangle piece of construction paper. Press it down onto the blue construction paper to the right of the oval. Make sure they are touching. Next, ask him to rub glue on the triangle piece. Place the triangle on top of the end of the rectangle. Rub glue on the quarter circle and place it on top of the oval, on the left side. Glue two craft sticks to look like an "X" above the oval. These will be the helicopter's propellers. Ask your toddler to glue some cotton balls in the sky to be clouds. Now he can use crayons to draw himself flying the helicopter.

Balloon Rockets

Materials:

- ☐ Balloons
- ☐ 6 Feet of Yarn
- ☐ Straw
- ☐ Tape
- ☐ Scissors
- ☐ 2 Chairs

Directions:

Ask your toddler if he wants to make a rocket. Rockets are a form of transportation that fly in the air. Cut a piece of yarn six feet or longer. Tie one end of the yarn to the back of a chair. Ask your toddler to thread a straw through the other end of the yarn. Tie the other end of the yarn to a second chair. Attach two pieces of tape, about two inches each, to the center of the straw. Leave the ends of the tape loose.

Now blow up a balloon. Leave the end untied, but hold the end so the air does not escape. Carefully attach the balloon to the tape and straw. Pull the balloon back to the chair closest to the opening of the balloon. Ask your toddler to hold the end of the balloon so that no air escapes. Count "1-2-3 blast off," and tell him to let go! We did this activity several times!

LOW PREP Air Counting

Materials:

- ☐ Air Counting Activity Page (Appendix AO)
- ☐ Crayons

Directions:

Show your toddler the *Air Counting* activity page. Tell him he will count the different forms of air transportation in the box, and then circle the correct number of items he counted.

For example, if there are three airplanes in one box your little one will count the number of airplanes he sees. Next, he will look at the numbers on the bottom of the box, find the three, and circle it with his crayon.

Water

LOW PREP Dot to Dot Boat

Materials:

- ☐ Dot to Dot Boat Activity Page (Appendix AP)
- ☐ Crayons

Directions:

Tell your toddler that some forms of transportation travel in the water. This is called water transportation. Tell them a few examples of water transportation. For example: sailboats, cargo boats, submarines, etc. Show him the *Dot to Dot Boat* activity page. Explain that he is going to connect the dots to make a picture. Show your toddler, with your finger, how he will use the numbers to go in order connecting the dots. You can have your toddler trace the dots with his finger first, and then give him a crayon to connect the dots. It helps if you count out loud together.

LOW PREP Build a Boat

Materials:

- ☐ Laundry Basket
- ☐ Pole
- ☐ Cardboard
- ☐ Scissors
- ☐ Crayons
- ☐ Tape

Directions:

Ask your toddler if he would like to make a boat he can sail in. Get out a laundry basket; a box also works. Now you need a pole. I used the pole from my broom, but a wrapping paper tube also works. Tape the pole, standing straight up, to the inside of the laundry basket. Make the sail by cutting out a right-angle triangle from a piece of cardboard or poster board. Ask your little one to decorate the sail on both sides. Now tape the sail to the pole. You and your toddler can sail away to a nice beach together!

Ice Boat Race

Materials:

- ☐ Small Cups
- ☐ Water
- ☐ Sticks (popsicle sticks, lollipop sticks, or straws)
- ☐ Aluminum Foil
- ☐ Paper
- ☐ Crayons
- ☐ Scissors
- ☐ Tape
- ☐ Pool Noodle
- ☐ Knife
- ☐ Bucket of Water
- ☐ Chair

Directions:

This activity may require a few hours because you have to wait for water to freeze. If you have a patient toddler, he can help you make boats, but if your toddler is inpatient, I recommend making the boats ahead of time. Start by filling up the small cups with an inch or two of water. I filled four small cups. Place a piece of aluminum foil on the top of each cup and press it down. Make a small slit in the center of the aluminum foil to slide your stick through. Place your stick in the hole. Now place your cups in the freezer.

Ask your toddler if he would like to have a boat race. Tell him he will need to make sails for the boats. Cut some diamond shapes out of paper. Let your toddler decorate the diamonds. While your toddler is decorating the sail, cut a pool noddle in half short and long ways. Pull your cups out of the freezer. Tell your toddler these will be the racing boats. Take the aluminum foil off each cup. Wrap the diamond around the stick so it forms a triangle sail. Tape it to the stick. Now take the boat out of the cup.

Set up your racing station by propping the pool noodle halves up on the edge of the chair. The bottom of the pool noodle should rest in a bucket of water. You can tape the noodles to the chair, if needed. You and your toddler should place your boats at the top of the pool noodle. Say, "1-2-3, go," to get the race started!

Submarine Snack

Materials:

- ☐ Hotdog Bun
- ☐ Peanut Butter
- ☐ Jelly
- ☐ 6 Blueberries
- ☐ Bendable Straw
- ☐ Knife
- ☐ Scissors

Directions:

Ask your toddler if he would like to make a submarine snack. Start by letting your toddler help you make a peanut butter and jelly sandwich on the hotdog bun. Spread a dollop of peanut butter onto each blueberry. Place three blueberries along the right side crease of the peanut butter and jelly sandwich. Spread them out to look like windows. Do the same for the left side of the sandwich. Cut the long end of a bendable straw to be four inches tall. Ask your toddler to stick the straw into the top of the sandwich and bend it back to look like the submarine's periscope. Now you have a submarine sandwich to enjoy!

All

Transportation Memory Game

Materials:

- ☐ Transportation Memory Game Activity Page (Appendix AQ)
- ☐ Scissors
- ☐ Tape (optional)
- ☐ Paper Plates (optional)

Directions:

Cut apart each square from the *Transportation Memory Game* activity pages. Show your toddler the different pictures of transportation. Tell him that you will turn all the pictures face down so he can't see them. It is best if you place them in a grid layout. Make sure they are in random order. Explain that he will get to pick one card to flip over. After he flips it over, ask him to try to find the match for that picture by flipping over another card. If he finds a match he gets to keep the cards and have another turn. If he does not get a match, he must return the cards and place them face down (make sure the cards stay in the same spots they were in) and it is mommy's turn.

If the cards are see through, you can tape them to the top of a paper plate and turn the paper plates face down.

LOW PREP Transportation Matching

Materials:

- ☐ Transportation Matching Activity Page (Appendix AR)
- ☐ Crayons

Directions:

Show your toddler the *Transportation Matching* activity page. Point to each picture of transportation, and ask him what it is. Ask your toddler where he would drive that mode of transportation. Now ask him to pick a crayon. Point to the first picture of transportation. Ask him what it is again. Ask your toddler if he sees a picture on the right-hand side of the activity page, where he would drive that mode of transportation. When he finds it, have him draw a line connecting the two pictures. Continue this until all the pictures are connected.

LOW PREP

Which One is Different?

Materials:

- ☐ Which One is Different? Activity Page (Appendix AS)
- ☐ Crayons

Directions:

Show your toddler the *Which One is Different* activity page, and ask him if he wants to find the different picture. Show him the first row. Tell him to look at all four pictures. Ask him if he sees one that is different from the rest. When he points it out, ask him to circle it with his crayon. Ask your toddler why it's different. Continue until he finds all the different pictures.

You can cut the rows apart to make it easier to identify the different picture, if needed.

Weather Activities

LOW PREP Rain Clouds

Materials:

- ☐ A Clear Vase
- ☐ Food Coloring
- ☐ Shaving Cream
- ☐ Eye Dropper, Syringe, or Measuring Spoon
- ☐ Water
- ☐ Small Bowls
- ☐ Spoon

Directions:

Ask your toddler if he wants to see how rain comes from clouds. Let your toddler pick two to three colors of food coloring. Get a small bowl for each color he picked. Pour a little bit (about ¼ cup) of water in each bowl. Then let your toddler add eight to ten drops of food coloring to each bowl. Stir it up.

Now fill your clear vase about two-thirds full of water. Squirt shaving cream generously over the top of the water. Explain to your toddler that the shaving cream is a cloud. Let your toddler use an eye dropper to drop the different colors of water onto the cloud. Tell your toddler that when the clouds start to get full of water that's when it starts to rain. See how long it takes before your cloud gets full and starts to rain.

LOW PREP Umbrella Bean Bag Toss

Materials:

- ☐ Umbrella
- ☐ Bean Bags

Directions:

Ask your toddler if he wants to play bean bag toss. Open an umbrella and lay it upside down so it looks like a bowl. Hand your toddler some bean bags. Make a line for him to stand behind, and tell him to toss the bean bags into the umbrella. See how many he can toss into the umbrella.

If you don't have bean bags you can make some by pouring some dried beans into a Ziploc bag. Seal the bag and place a piece of tape over the seal.

LOW PREP

Cloud Play

Materials:

- ☐ Shaving Cream

Directions:

Ask your toddler if he wants to play in clouds. Squirt a bunch of shaving cream on the table and let him have fun squishing it between his fingers, drawing in it, and smearing it around. You can practice writing letters, numbers, drawing lines, etc. A nice bonus of this activity is that the shaving cream will clean your table.

LOW PREP

Make Lightning

Materials:

- ☐ Balloon
- ☐ Metal Spoon

Directions:

Ask your toddler if he wants to make lightning. Blow up a balloon. Ask your toddler to rub the balloon on his hair or carpet for two minutes. Turn the lights off to make the room dark. Touch the spoon to the balloon. You should see a small spark when the two meet. Your toddler will probably want to do this activity a couple of times!

LOW PREP Make an Anemometer

Materials:

- ☐ 4 Straws
- ☐ 4 Small Paper Cups
- ☐ Tape
- ☐ Straight Pin
- ☐ Nail
- ☐ Single Hole Punch
- ☐ New Pencil

Directions:

Ask your toddler if he wants to make an anemometer. Tell him an anemometer measures how fast the wind is blowing. See if your toddler can stick one straw end into another straw end to make a long straw. Do this with the two other straws. You should now have two long straws. Punch two holes in each cup—make sure the holes are in a straight line. Now ask your toddler to slide a cup onto each end of the long straw.

Cross the two long straws to make an "X." Attach them with tape. Make sure all cup openings are facing the same direction. Use a nail to make a hole in the center of the "X." Take the nail out and stick a straight pin through the hole and into the eraser of your pencil. Test out the anemometer by going outside to see if it spins!

LOW PREP Make a Rain Stick

Materials:

- ☐ Cylinder (ex. Pringles can, bread crumb tube, etc.)
- ☐ Tape
- ☐ Hammer
- ☐ Nails
- ☐ Dried Beans
- ☐ Rice
- ☐ Noodles

Directions:

Ask your toddler if he wants to make a rain stick. Explain to your toddler that he will get to use a hammer for this activity. Remind him that hammers only hit nails. Explain to your toddler that hammers are only to be used when mommy or daddy is around. Let your toddler use the hammer to nail in nails randomly around the cylinder container. The more nails the better the rain stick will sound.

When he finishes hammering the nails let your toddler add as much rice, dried beans, and noodles as he would like, but you don't want him to fill it all the way up. Place the top on the container. Tape the top on to help it stay closed. My sons were so excited to play with their rain stick they didn't want to decorate it, but you can let your toddler decorate his rain stick if he would like.

Weather Station

Materials:

- ☐ Weather Station Activity Page (Appendix AT)
- ☐ Crayons
- ☐ Scissors
- ☐ Glue
- ☐ Brass Fastener
- ☐ Cardstock
- ☐ Paper Plate

Directions:

Ask your toddler if he wants to make a weather station where he will be able to show the weather every day. Show him the *Weather Station* activity page. Point to each picture of weather and talk about what it is. Let your toddler color each weather picture. While he is coloring cut out the arrow from the activity page and trace it onto a piece of cardstock. Cut out the arrow from cardstock.

When your toddler finishes coloring you can help him cut out the weather station. You want to cut out the full circle. Then ask your toddler to glue the weather station onto a paper plate. Place a small slit in the center of the plate. Place a small slit in the end of the arrow. Place the arrow slit on top of the paper plate slit and slide a brass fastener through it. Ask your toddler to look outside to see what the weather is like today. Then have him move the arrow to the correct weather station. You can do this each day!

LOW PREP Make a Tornado

Materials:

- ☐ 2 Empty Soda Bottles
- ☐ Duct Tape
- ☐ Water

Directions:

Ask your toddler if he wants to make a tornado. If you are like us and don't drink soda, you can use two empty water bottles—just make sure the bottles are the same size. Ask your toddler to help you fill one bottle two-thirds full of water. Place the empty bottle directly on top of the bottle with water. Connect them by wrapping them tightly with duct tape. Now ask your toddler to quickly turn the bottles over and set it on a table. If the water doesn't start to form a tornado then ask your toddler to swirl it around to get the tornado started.

Weather Sensory Bin

Materials:

- ☐ Bucket
- ☐ Rice
- ☐ Toy Sun or Sun Print Out
- ☐ White or Yellow Pipe Cleaners
- ☐ Cotton Balls
- ☐ Blue Marbles
- ☐ Foam or Confetti Snowflakes

Directions:

Fill a bucket with rice. Place the toy sun, cotton balls (clouds), blue marbles (raindrops), and snowflakes in the rice. Take the pipe cleaners and bend them to look like a lightning bolt. Place the lightning bolts in the rice. You can bury all the weather materials if you'd like.

Ask your toddler if he would like to dig for different weather things. Place the bucket in front of him and ask him to find things. When he finds something ask him to guess what weather thing it might be.

Count Snowballs

Materials:

- ☐ Snowball Counting Activity Page (Appendix AU)
- ☐ White Pom Poms or Cotton Balls
- ☐ Muffin Tin
- ☐ Tongs (optional)

Directions:

You will need to cut out the circle numbers from the *Snowball Counting* activity page. Place each number in the bottom of a muffin tin cup. Make sure you put the numbers in order. Ask your toddler if he would like to count snowballs. Place the muffin tin in front of him along with the pom poms. Start with number "1," ask him what number it is. When he tells you, ask him how many snowballs he needs to put in the cup. He can use his fingers or tongs to place the snowballs in the cup. Continue until all 12 cups are full.

Zoo Animal Activities

LOW PREP Animal Cracker Counting

Materials:

- ☐ Animal Crackers
- ☐ Index Cards
- ☐ Marker

Directions:

Ask your toddler if he wants to count the animals in the zoo. Write numbers 1-10 on index cards. If your toddler is more advanced at number recognition and counting, you can write 1-15 or 1-20 on index cards. There should be one number for each card. Place the index cards in front of your toddler, in numerical order. Point to each card and say the number with your toddler. Start at "1," and ask your toddler what number it is. Ask him how many animal crackers he needs to put on the card. Continue until he has filled all his cards.

LOW PREP Animal Movements

Materials:

- ☐ Animal Movement Activity Page (Appendix AV)
- ☐ Scissors

Directions:

Ask your toddler if he wants to pretend to be animals. Cut apart the animal movement cards. Put the cards in a hat. Let your toddler pull a card out of the hat. Read what the card says to do, and instruct him what movement to do. It's fun to pretend to be the animals with him!

Mixed Up Chameleon

Materials:

- ☐ Ziploc Bag
- ☐ Marker
- ☐ 2 Paint Colors
- ☐ Tape

Directions:

Draw a chameleon on a Ziploc bag. I looked one up online to see how to draw it; it doesn't have to be perfect. Squirt a glob of paint in one corner of the bag and a glob of paint in the other corner. You want to choose from the primary colors, so yellow and blue, yellow and red, or red and blue. Tape the chameleon to a table or counter top.

Ask your toddler if he wants to paint a chameleon. Show him the chameleon you drew. Explain that chameleons can change colors to match the surface it is on so it can hide from animals that might eat the chameleon. Explain that he will mix the two colors together to try to change the chameleon's color.

Elephant Trunk Scoot

Materials:

- ☐ Long Balloon
- ☐ Tape
- ☐ Ping Pong Balls

Directions:

Ask your toddler if he wants to pretend to be an elephant. You will need to blow up a long balloon, the kind you use to make balloon animals. Tape a square down on the floor. Throw a few ping pong balls onto the floor. Tell your toddler to hold the balloon at his nose like an elephant trunk. Next, tell him to swing his trunk around on the ground to try to move the ping pong balls into the square.

LOW PREP Giraffe Spots

Materials:

- ☐ Giraffe Spots Activity Page (Appendix AW)
- ☐ Cheerios

Directions:

Tell your toddler the giraffe is missing his spots, and he needs his help to get his spots back. Show him the *Giraffe Spots* activity page. Place Cheerios in front of him. Explain to your toddler that you will call out a letter. Next, he has to find the letter, and put a Cheerio on it in order to give the giraffe back his spot. Call the letters out in ABC order.

Make a Cheetah Mask

Materials:

- ☐ Paper Plate
- ☐ Craft Stick
- ☐ Yellow and Black Paint
- ☐ Paintbrush
- ☐ Scissors
- ☐ Tape
- ☐ Yellow Construction Paper
- ☐ Glue

Directions:

Ask your toddler if he wants to make a cheetah mask. First, you will need to cut out two holes in the paper plate for your toddler's eyes. Let him use a paintbrush to paint the entire mask yellow. While he is painting you can cut out two ears from the yellow construction paper for the cheetah. After your toddler is finished painting the plate yellow, let him use his finger to dip in the black paint and put spots all over the cheetah mask. He can also use the black paint to add a nose and mouth. Let the paint dry.

When the paint has dried, let your toddler glue the ears to the top of the mask. Flip the mask over, and tape a craft stick to the bottom of the mask to use as a handle. Ta-da, now you have a cheetah!

Monkey Snack

Materials:

- ☐ Slice of Bread
- ☐ Nutella
- ☐ 2 Banana Slices
- ☐ 2 Blueberries

Directions:

Ask your toddler if he wants to make a "monkey snack." Toast a piece of bread. Let your toddler spread Nutella across the toast. Let your toddler place two blueberries on the upper half of the bread, where you would place eyes.

Cut two slices of banana in half—they should look like half moons. Ask your toddler to place one half moon under the eyes with the curved part under the blueberries. Next, ask your toddler to place one half moon under the banana with the curved part pointed towards the bottom of the bread. This is the monkey's nose and mouth. Ask your toddler to place one half moon to the right of the blueberries with the curved part facing the crust of the toast. Now your toddler can place the last half moon on the left side of the toast. These are the monkey's ears. Enjoy your monkey snack!

Appendix

If you need extra copies of the appendix pages,
please visit this link to download more appendix pages:

www.bestmomideas.com/sendmyultimateprintouts

Password: bestmomideas6p75

cut along line

cut along line

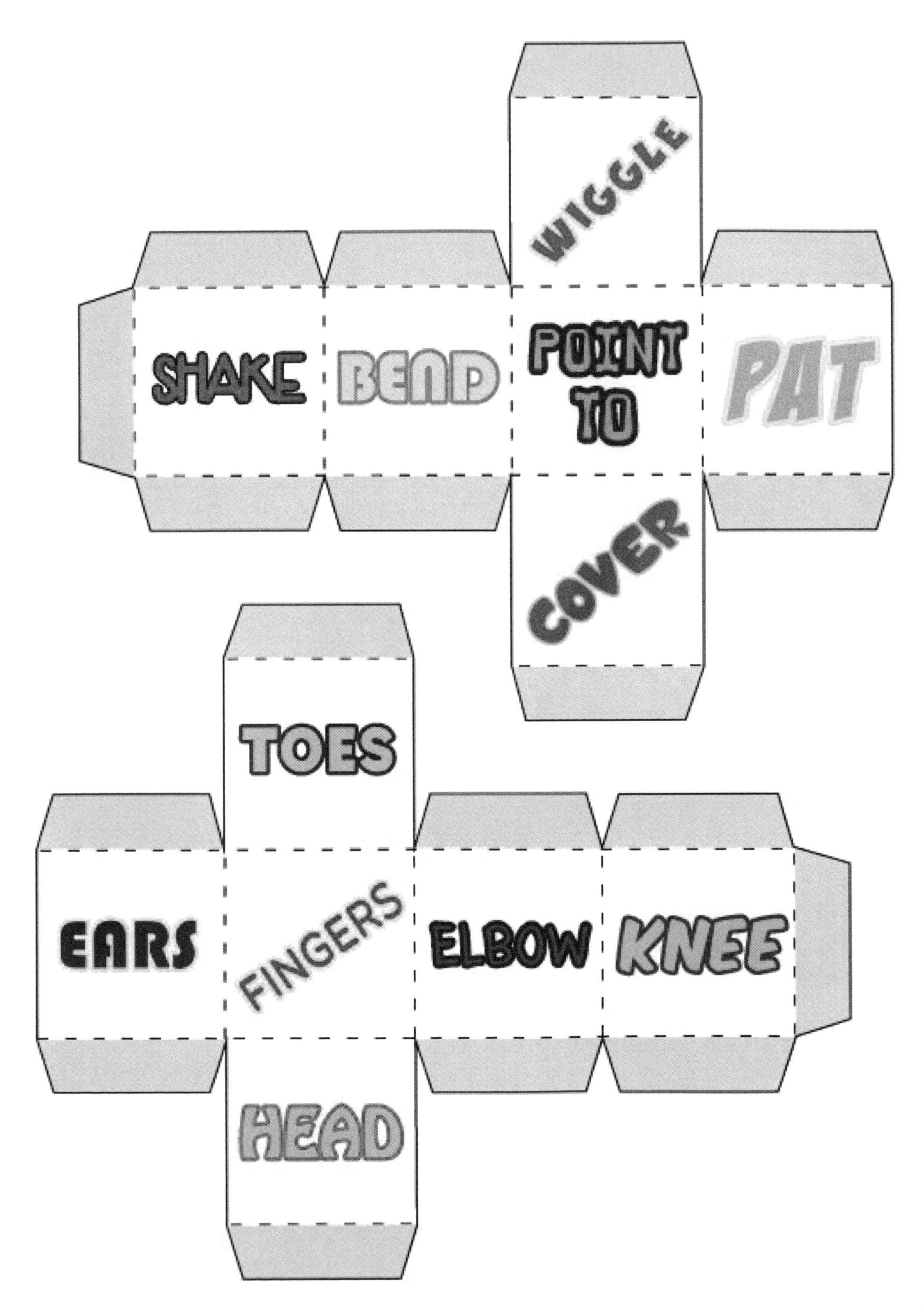

cut along line

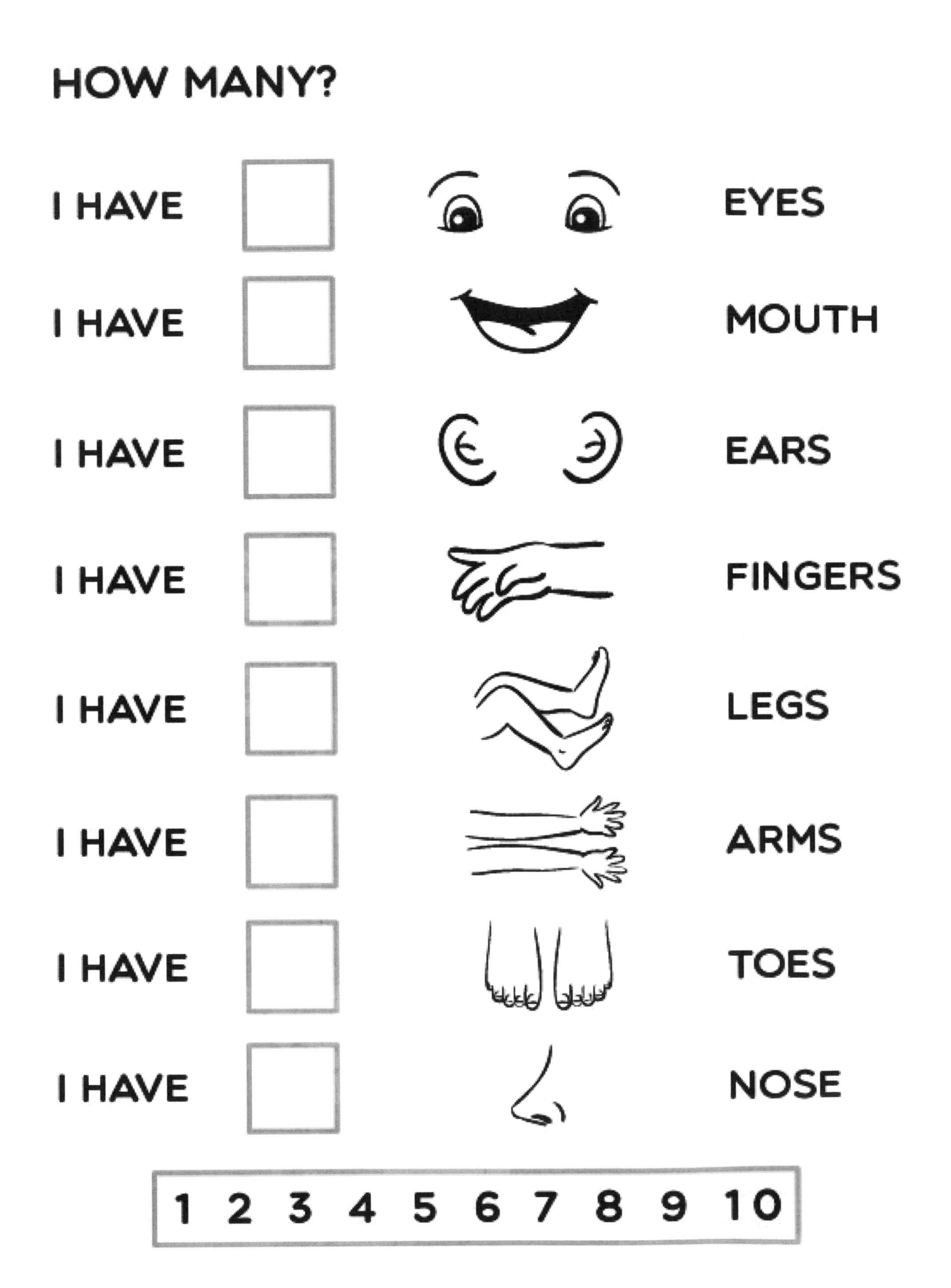

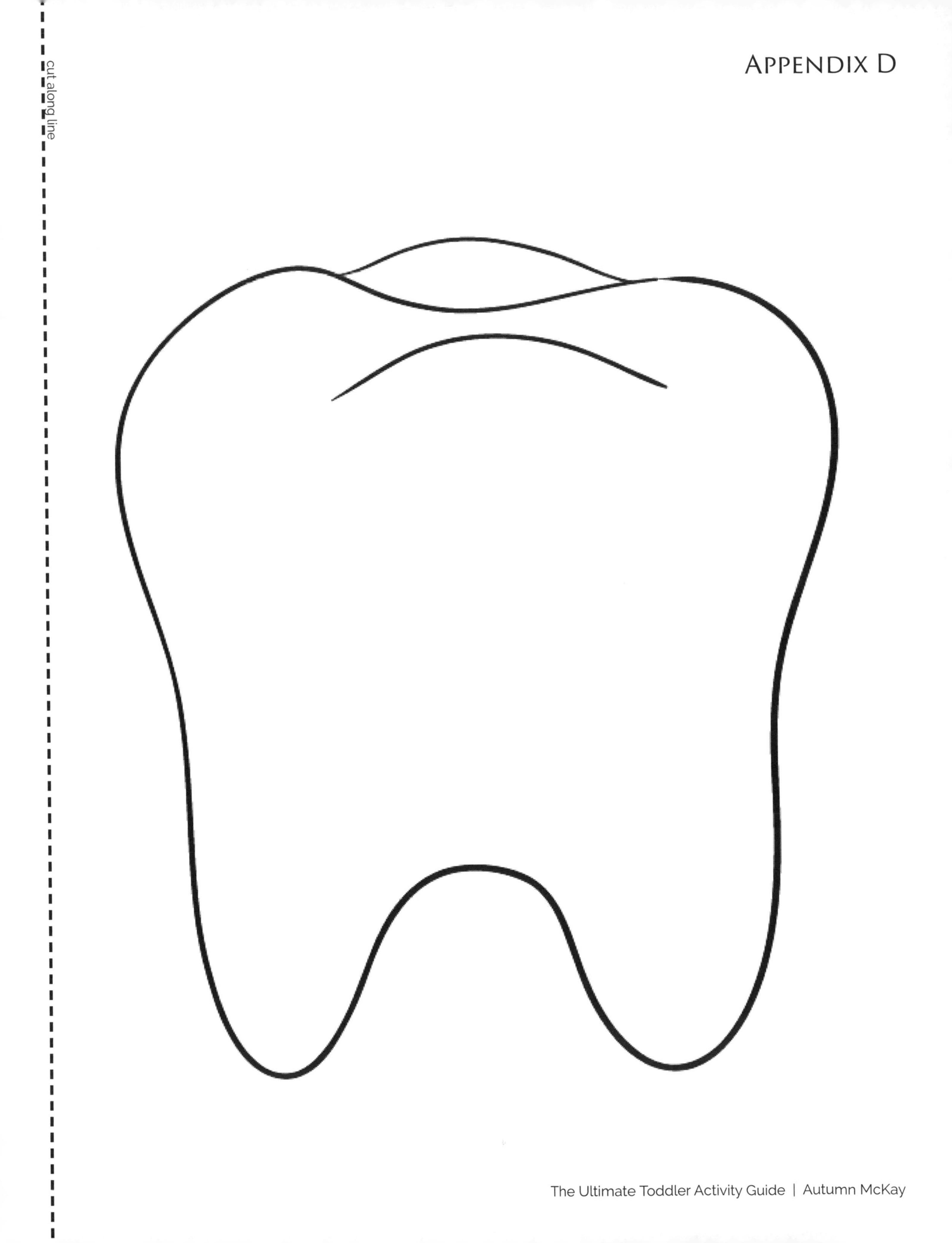
cut along line

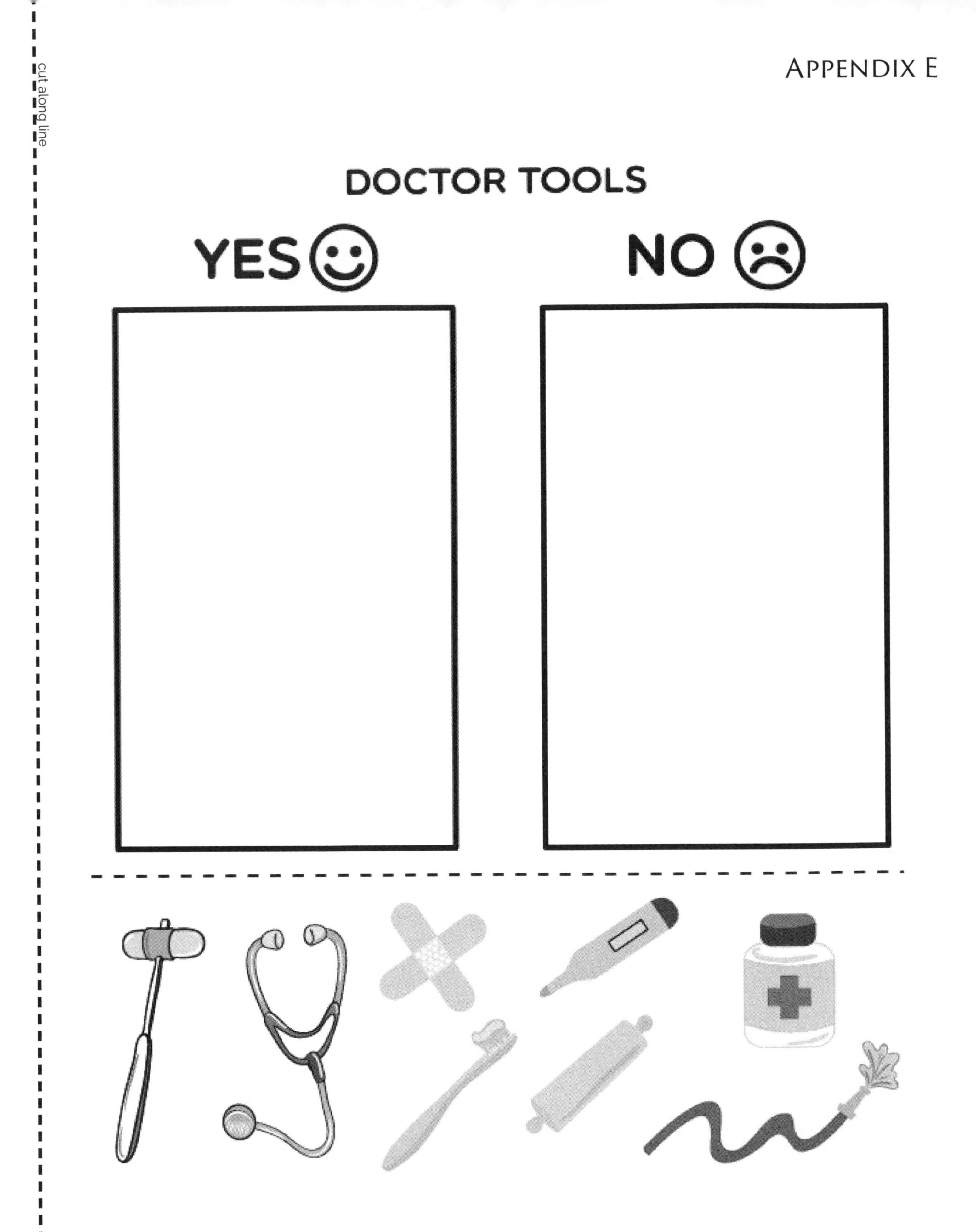
cut along line
DOCTOR TOOLS
YES
NO

cut along line

cut along line
911

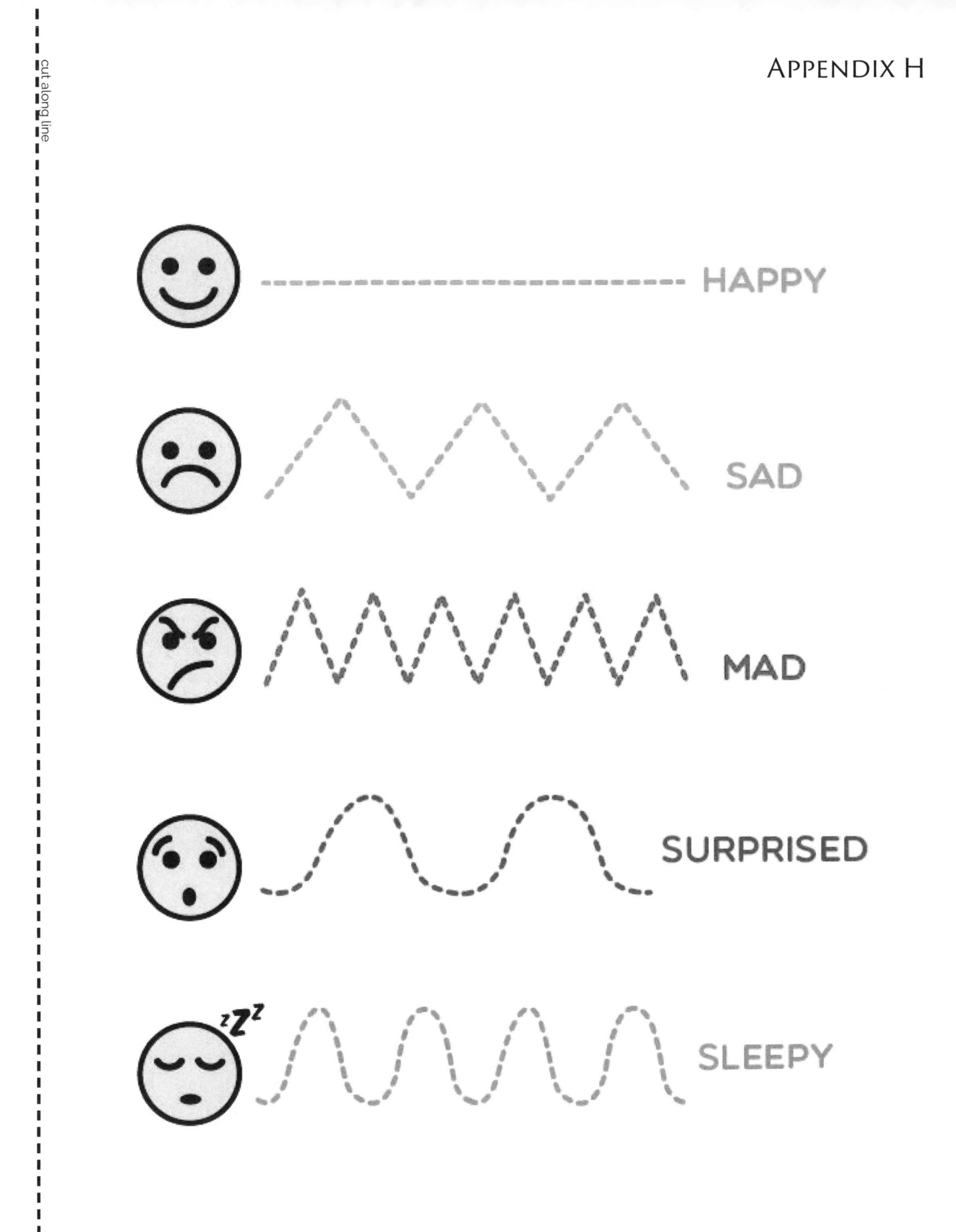
cut along line
HAPPY
SAD
MAD
SURPRISED
SLEEPY

cut along line

RIGHT NOW I'M FEELING

cut along line

cut along line

cut along line

MARTIN LUTHER KING JR. WANTED EVERYONE TO BE TREATED

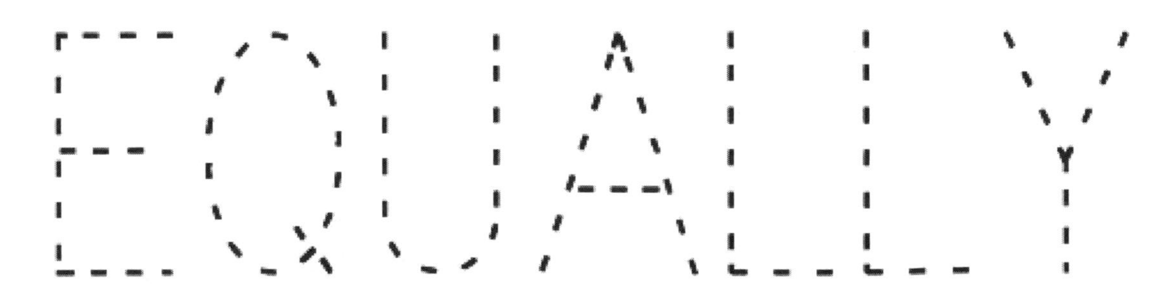

cut along line
I HAVE A
DREAM

APPENDIX N

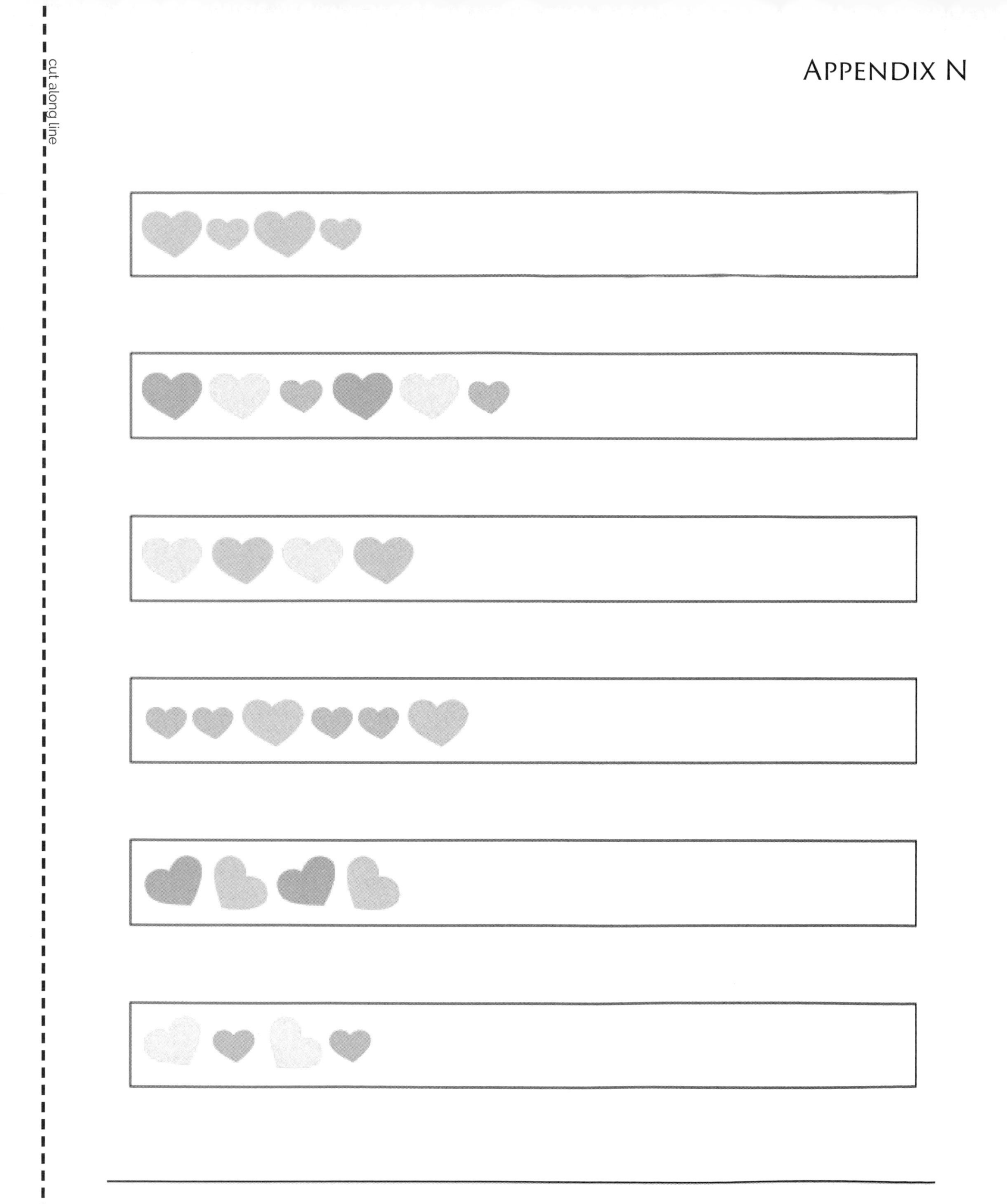

cut along line

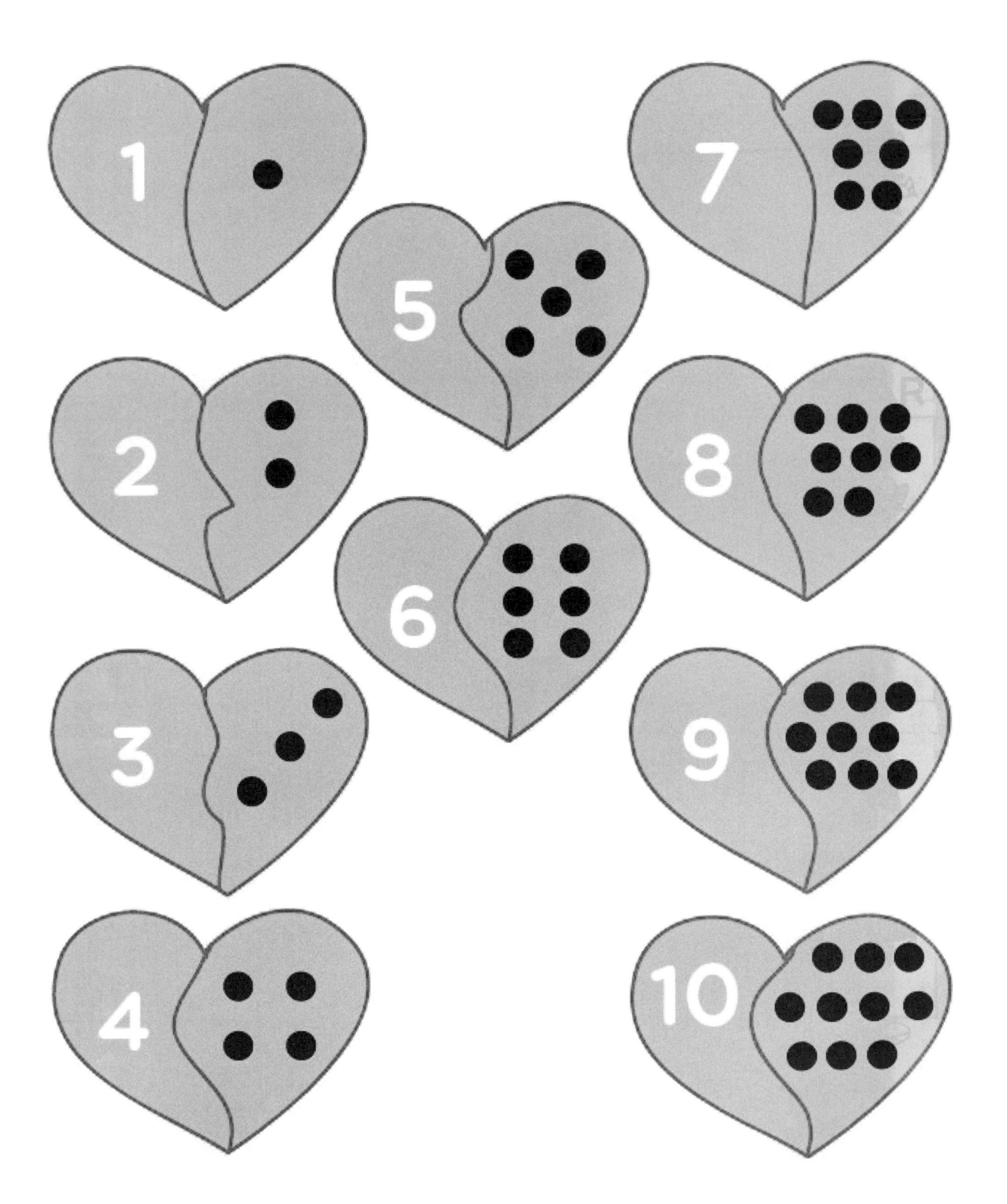

cut along line

1 BLACK 2 YELLOW 3 RED
4 BLUE 5 GRAY 6 ORANGE

GIVE YOUR CHILD THE FOLLOWING GUIDELINES TO COLLECT THINGS THAT ARE GREEN.
AS ITEMS ARE FOUND, MARK THEM OFF WITH A GREEN CRAYON.

FIND SOMETHING THAT GROWS GREEN.

FIND SOMETHING SOFT THAT IS GREEN.

FIND ONE SNACK ITEM THAT IS GREEN.

NAME ONE ANIMAL THAT IS GREEN.

FIND SOMETHING HARD THAT IS GREEN.

NAME A FRUIT THAT IS GREEN.

FIND SOMETHING YOU PLAY WITH THAT IS GREEN,

FIND SOMETHING YOU CAN COLOR WITH THAT IS GREEN.

FIND SOMETHING YOU CAN BUILD WITH THAT IS GREEN.

FIND SOMETHING ON A WALL THAT IS GREEN.

FIND SOMETHING YOU CAN WEAR THAT IS GREEN.

cut along line

E

GOD LOVES EVERYONE!

A IS FOR A BROKEN WORLD

PEOPLE MADE BOO-BOOS AND MESSED UP, BUT JESUS LOVES US SO MUCH THAT HE HELPED FIX THOSE MESS UPS.

S IS FOR SACRIFICE

JESUS DIED ON THE CROSS FOR US SO THAT WE COULD BE WITH HIM IN HEAVEN ONE DAY!

T IS FOR TOMB

AFTER JESUS DIED, HE WAS BURIED IN A TOMB (it's like a cave) WITH A BIG ROCK IN FRONT OF THE DOOR.
HE STAYED THERE FOR 3 DAYS.

E IS FOR EMPTY

WHEN JESUS' FRIENDS WENT TO VISIT HIM AT THE TOMB THEY SAW THAT THE BIG ROCK HAD BEEN ROLLED AWAY AND THE TOMB WAS EMPTY.
JESUS' CLOTHES WERE FOLDED UP NICELY.

R IS FOR RISEN

JESUS ROSE FROM THE DEAD! HE NOW LIVES IN HEAVEN WITH GOD. AND WE CAN TALK, SING, AND PRAY TO HIM TODAY!

LUKE 23

cut along line

SORTING TRASH

CUT THE PICTURES AT THE BOTTOM AND PASTE THEM IN THE RIGHT CATEGORY.

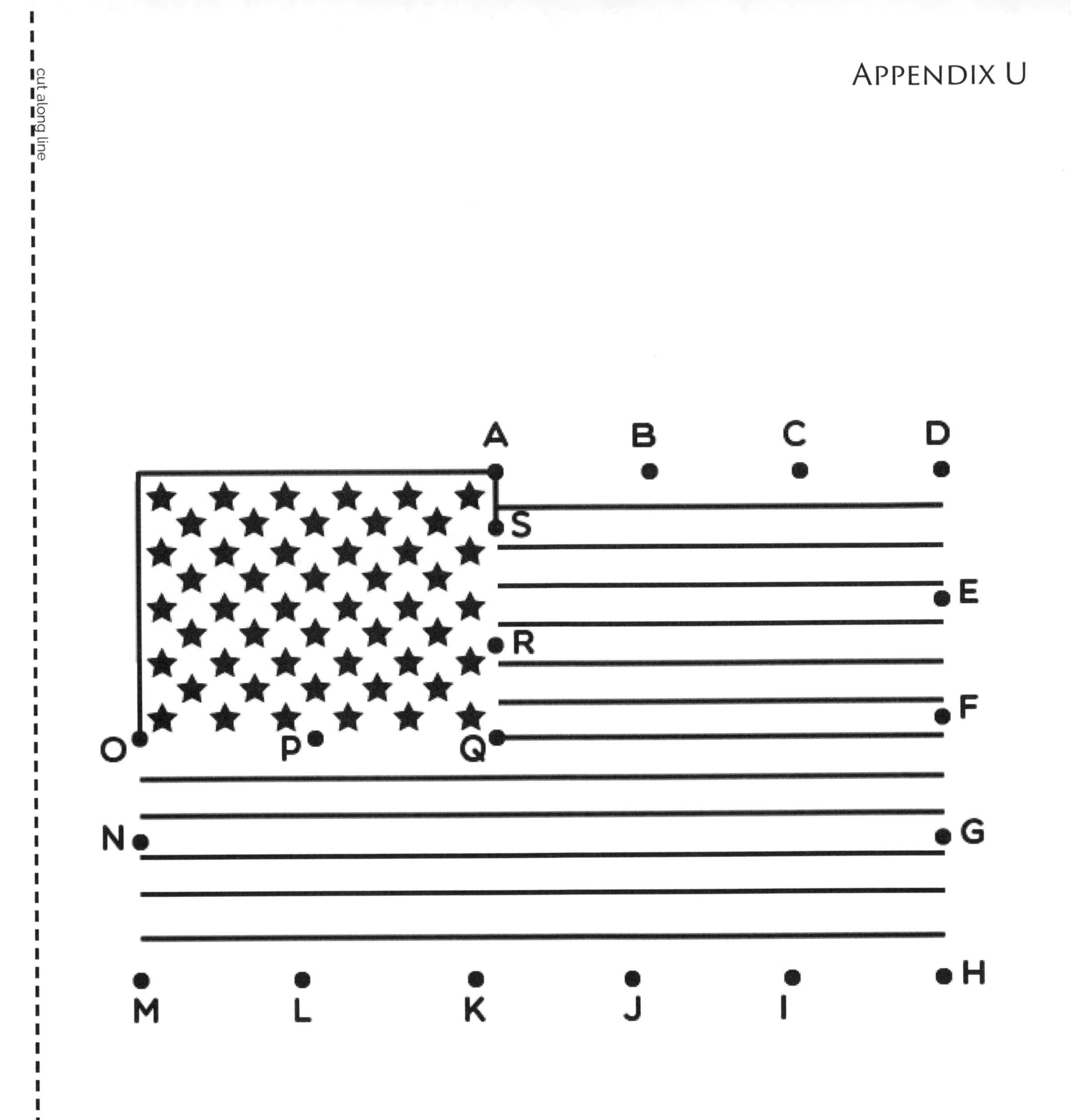
cut along line
A
B
C
D
S
E
R
F
O
P
Q
N
G
H
M
L
K
J
I

cut along line

APPENDIX V

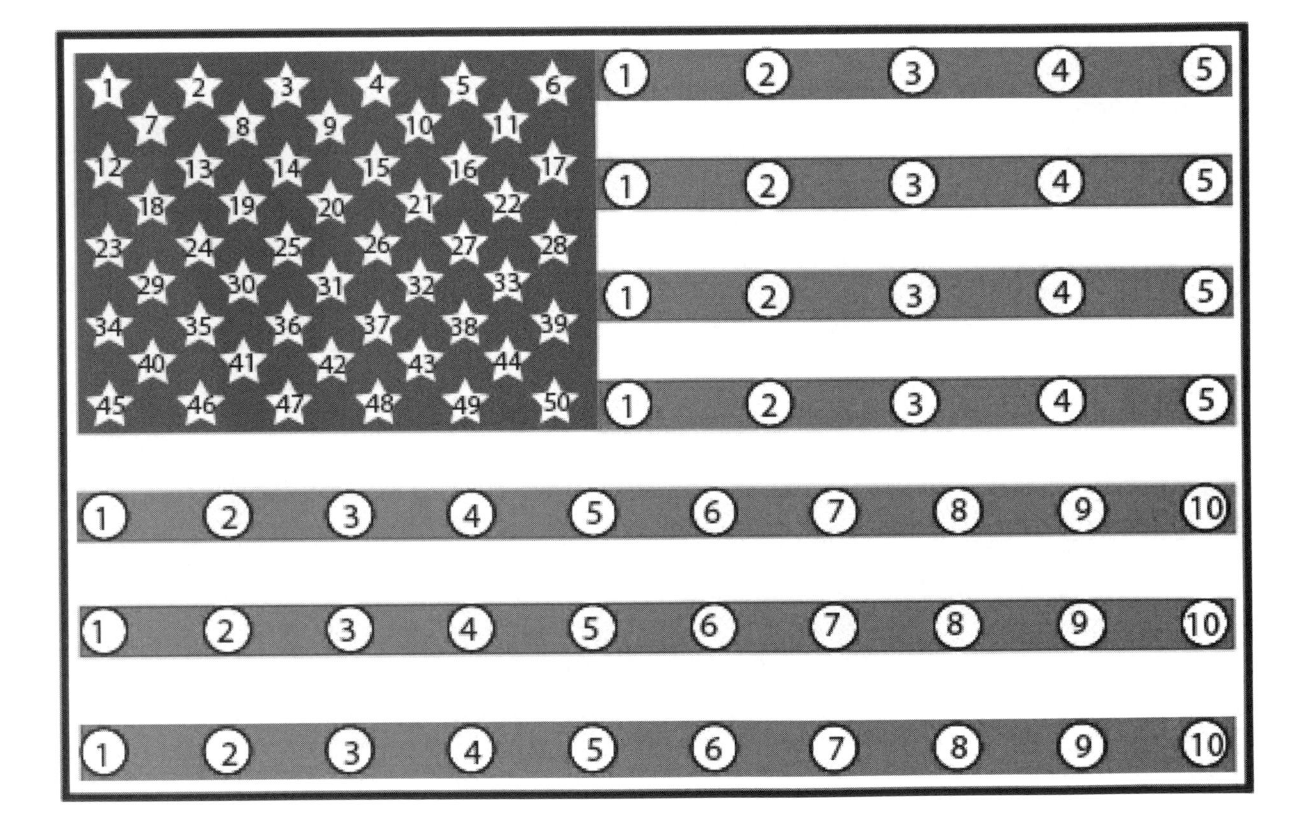

cut along line

HOW MANY STARS?

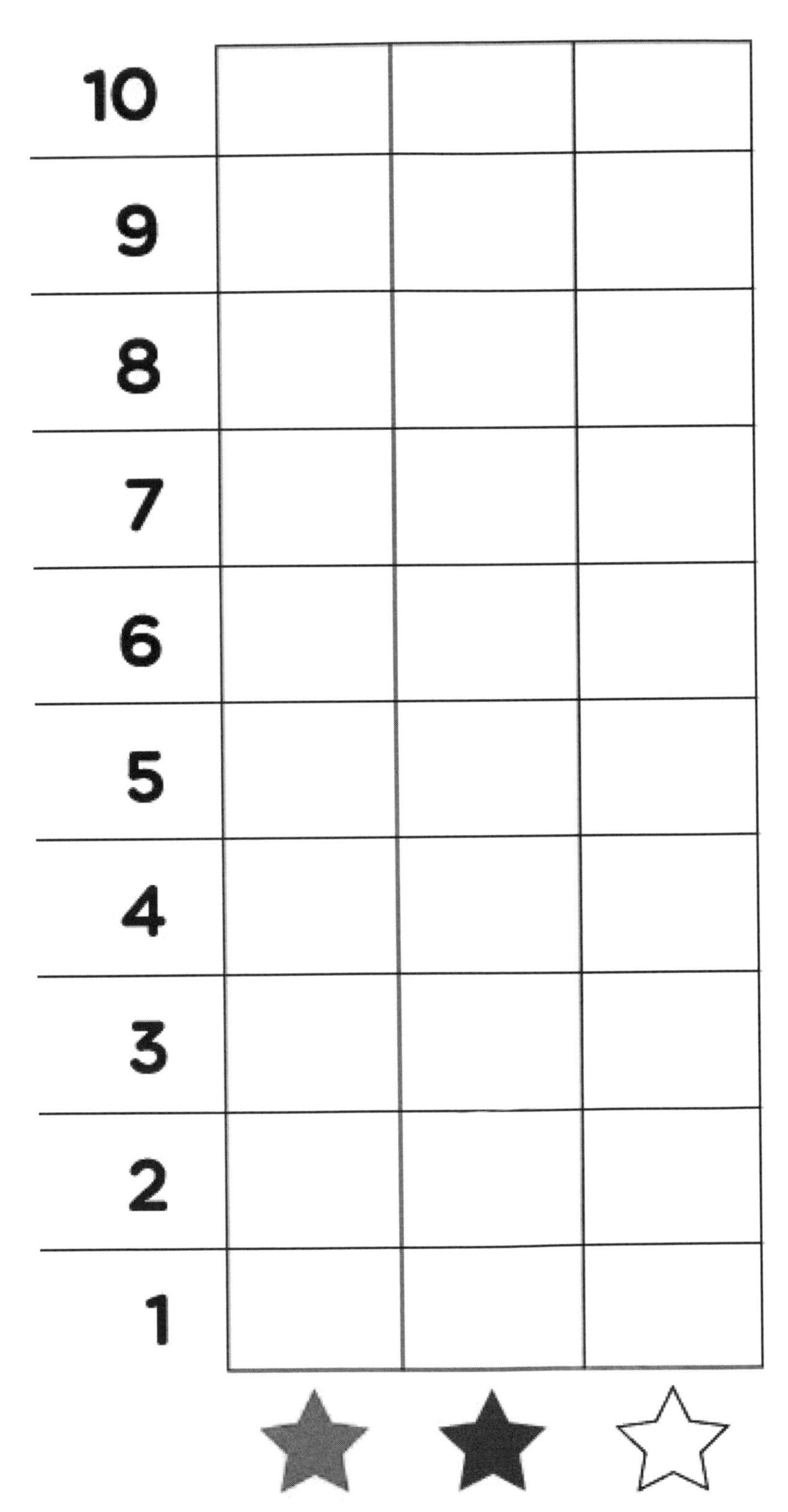

cut along line

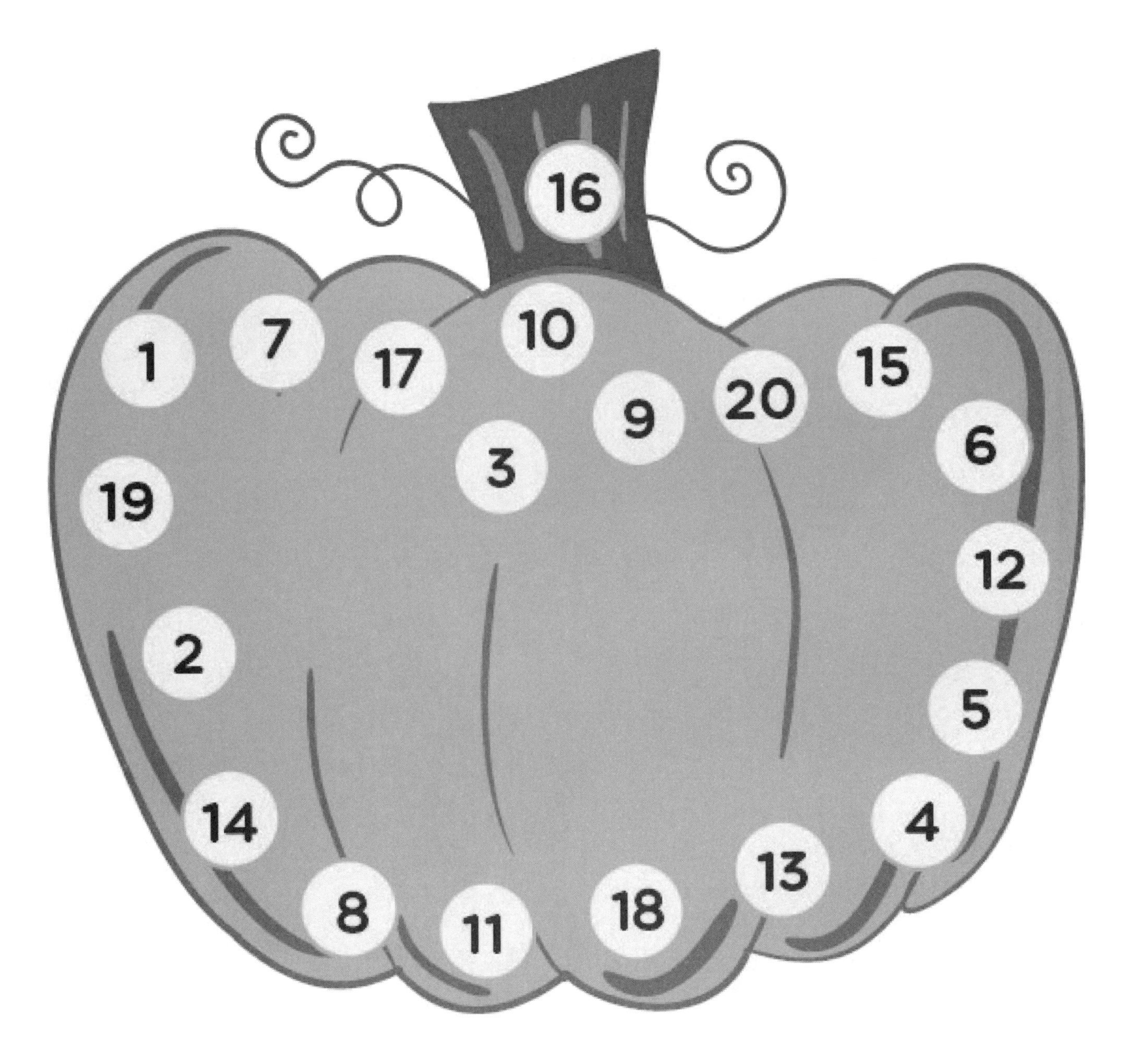

cut along line

cut along line

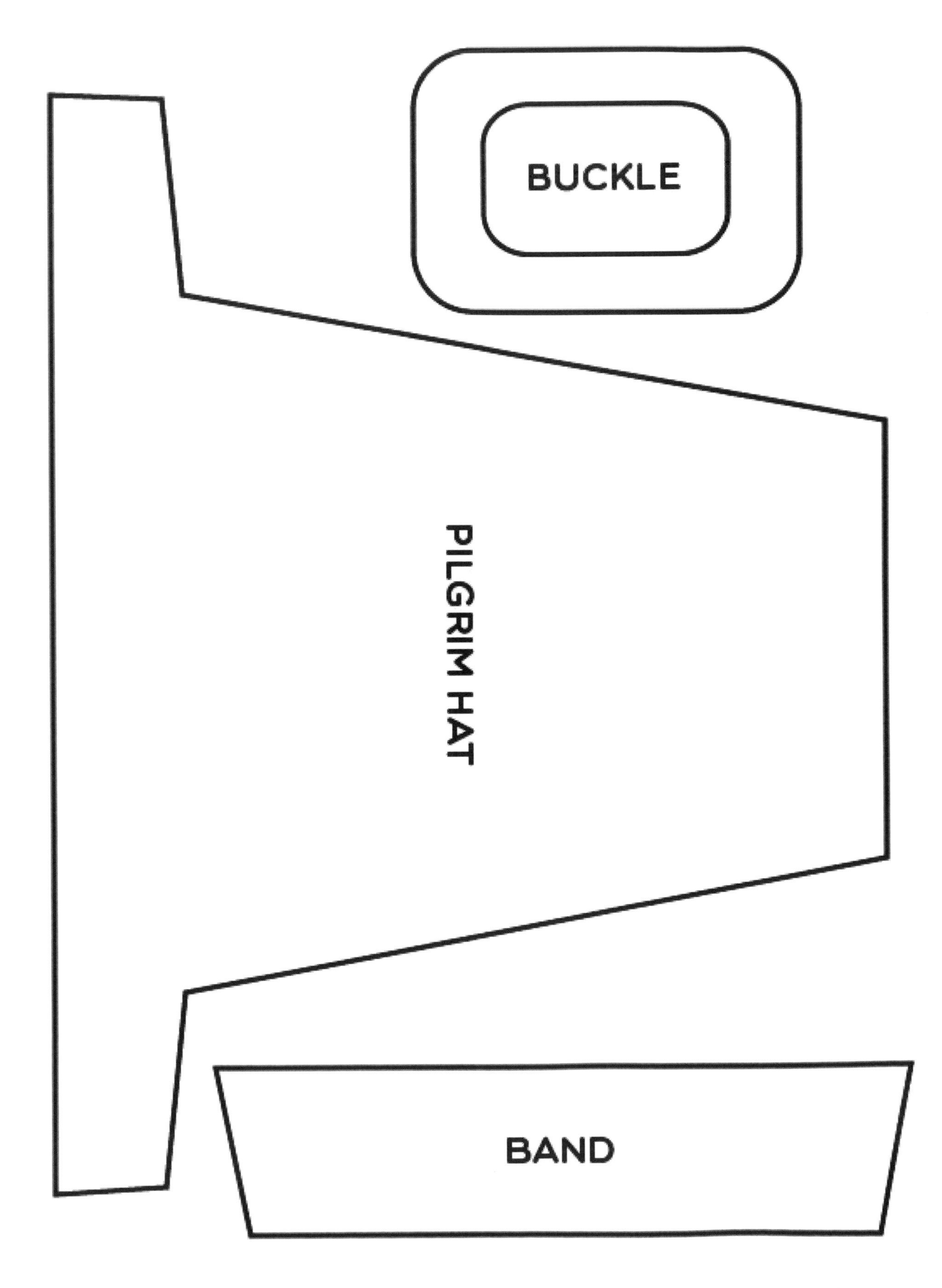

cut along line

HAPPY THANKSGIVING!!

NATIVITY COLOR BY NUMBER

1- BLUE 2- BROWN 3-SKIN 4-YELLOW
5- ORANGE 6- WHITE

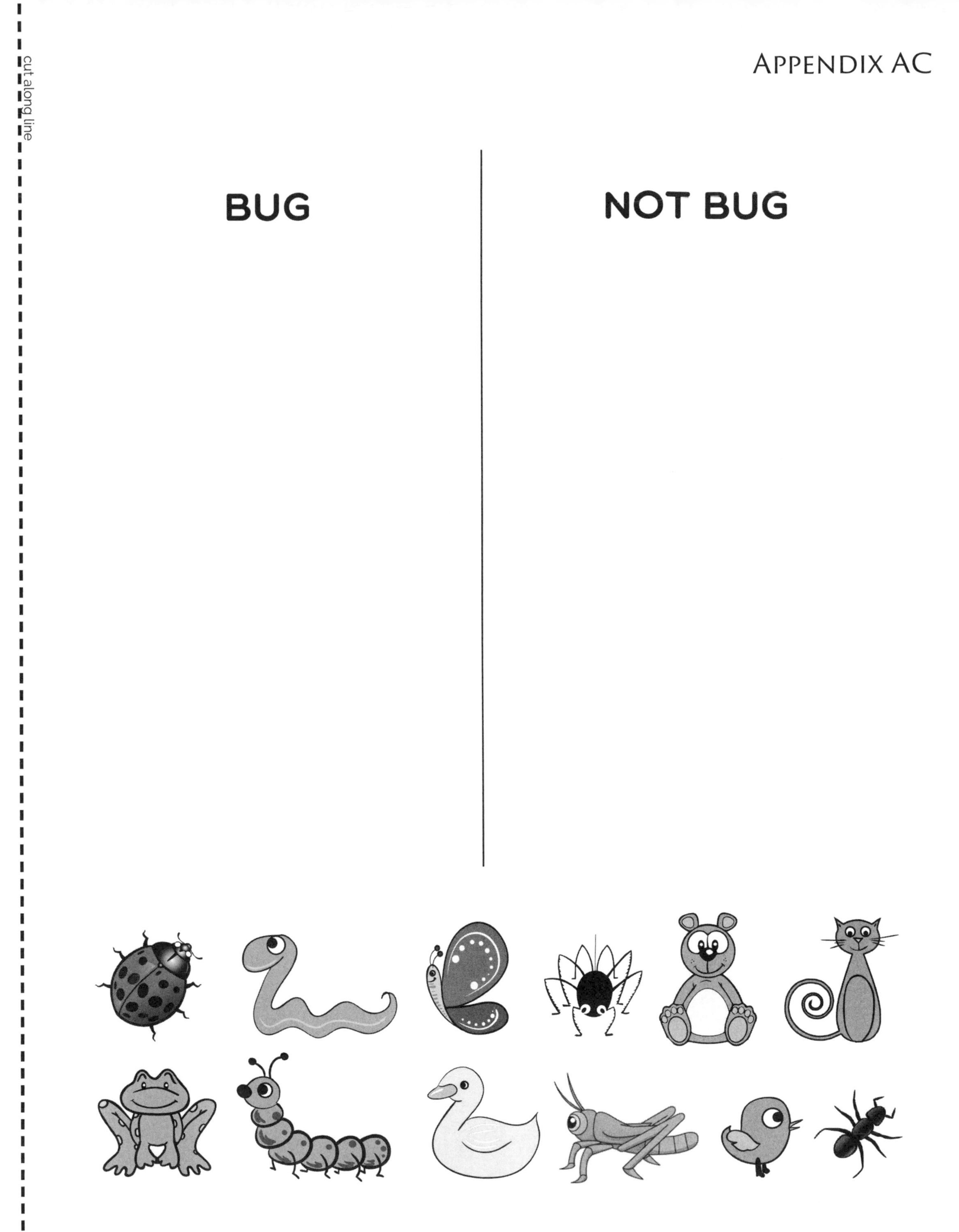
cut along line
BUG
NOT BUG

cut along line

CATERPILLAR COUNTING

cut along line

BUG WALK

ANT SPIDER CATERPILLAR

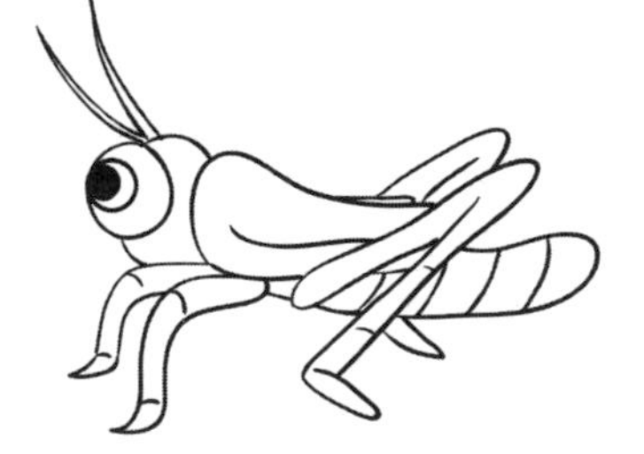

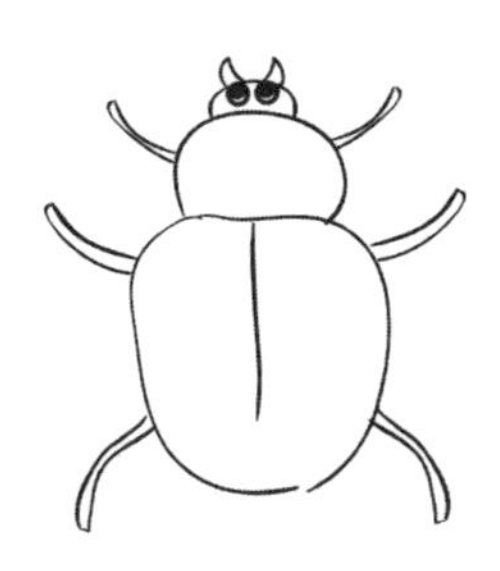

BUTTERFLY GRASSHOPPER BEETLE

LADYBUG

cut along line

LEFT AND RIGHT

COLOR THE LEFT HAND

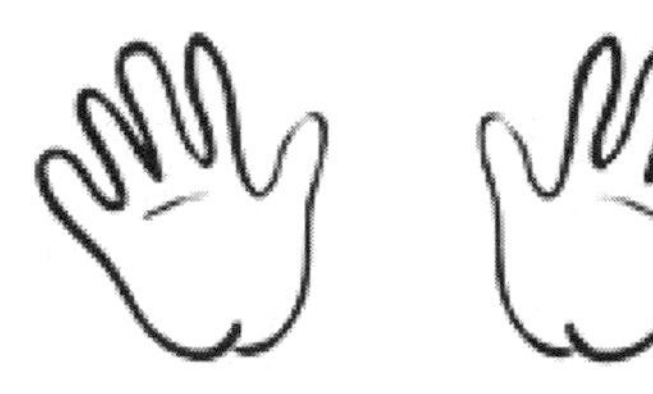

COLOR THE RIGHT FOOT

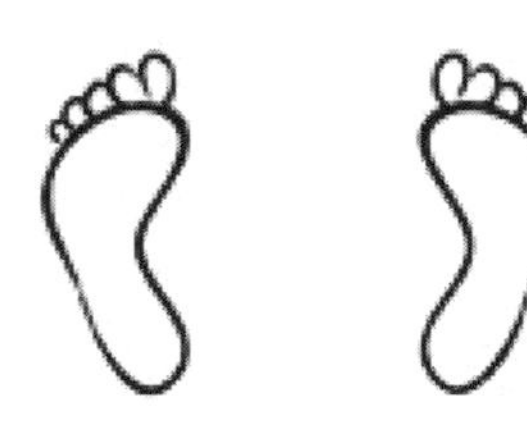

COLOR THE LEFT LEAF

COLOR THE LEFT HEART

COLOR THE RIGHT HAND

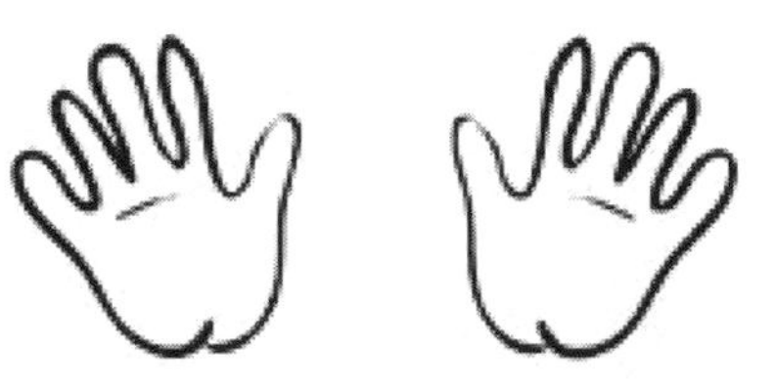

COLOR THE LEFT FOOT

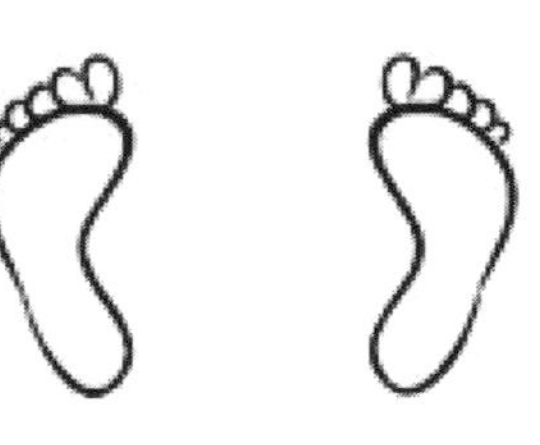

COLOR THE RIGHT BUTTERFLY

COLOR THE RIGHT FLOWER

cut along line

WHERE DO WE LIVE?

GLUE THE LIVING CREATURES ON THE CORRECT HABITAT

OCEAN

cut along line

cut along line

FALL	SUMMER	SPRING	WINTER

cut along line

cut along line

MATCH YOUR FIVE SENSES

cut along line

Appendix AL (2)

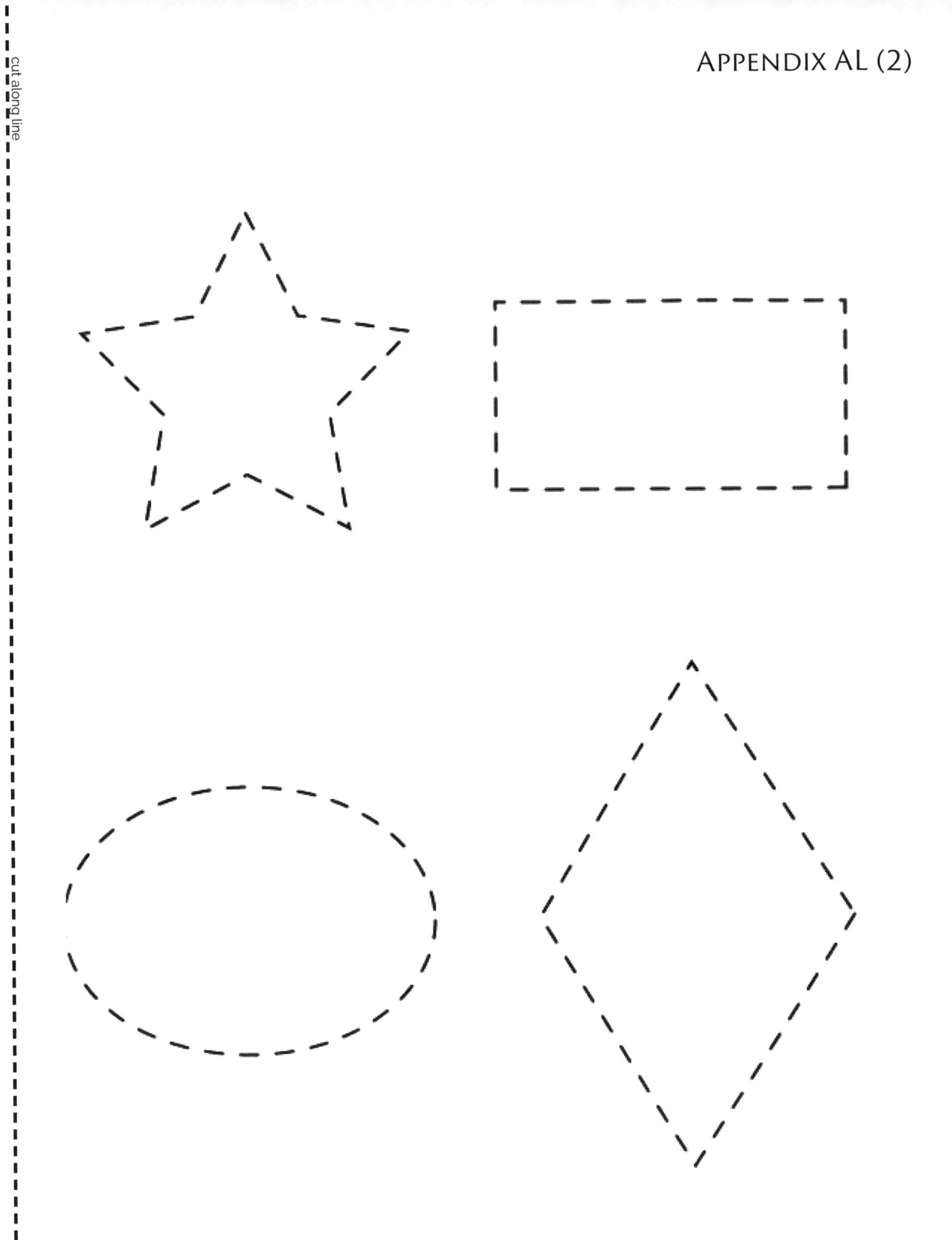

cut along line

cut along line

STAR SEARCH

cut along line

WEATHER BEAR

cut along line

cut along line

cut along line

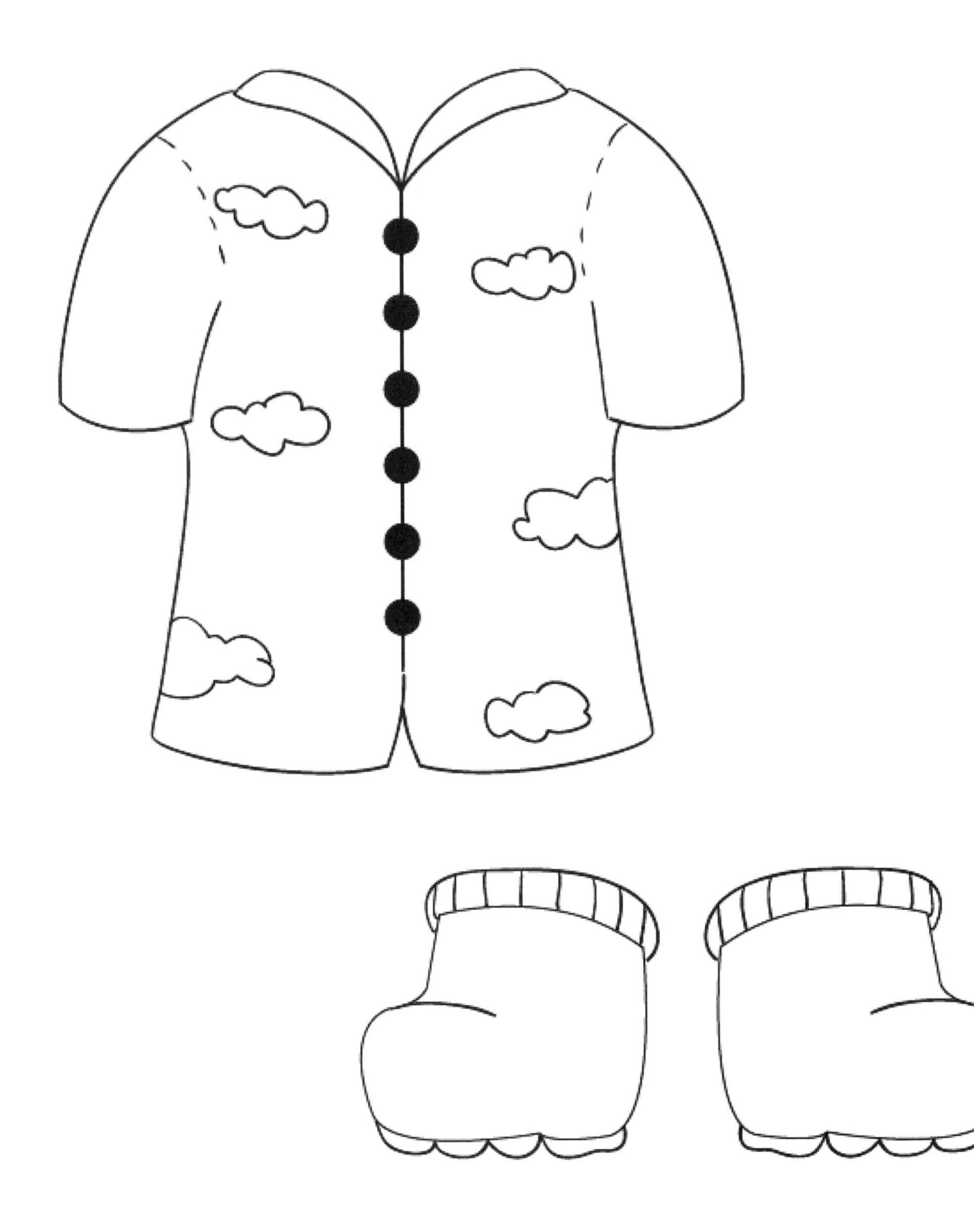

Appendix AO

cut along line

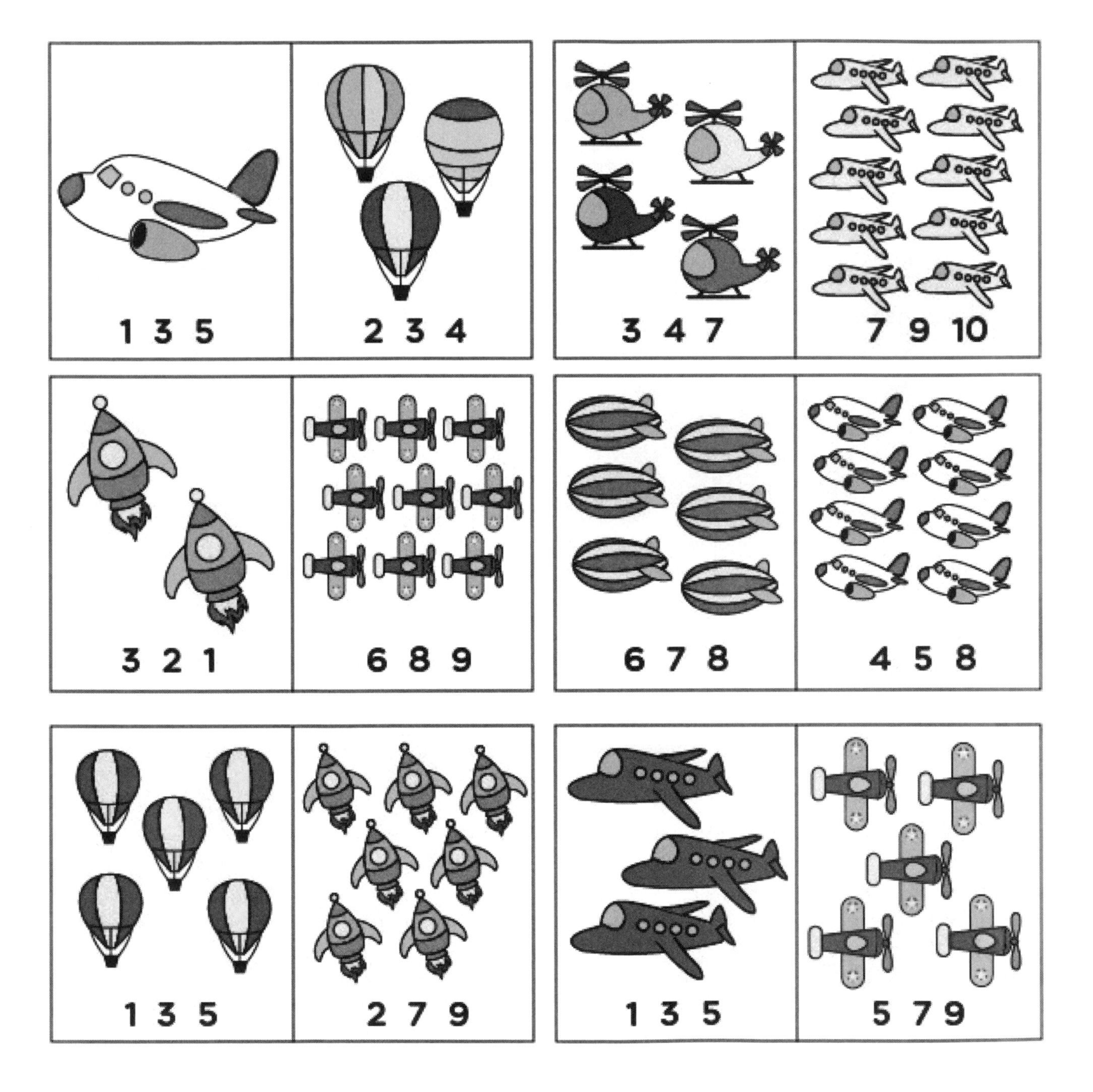

cut along line

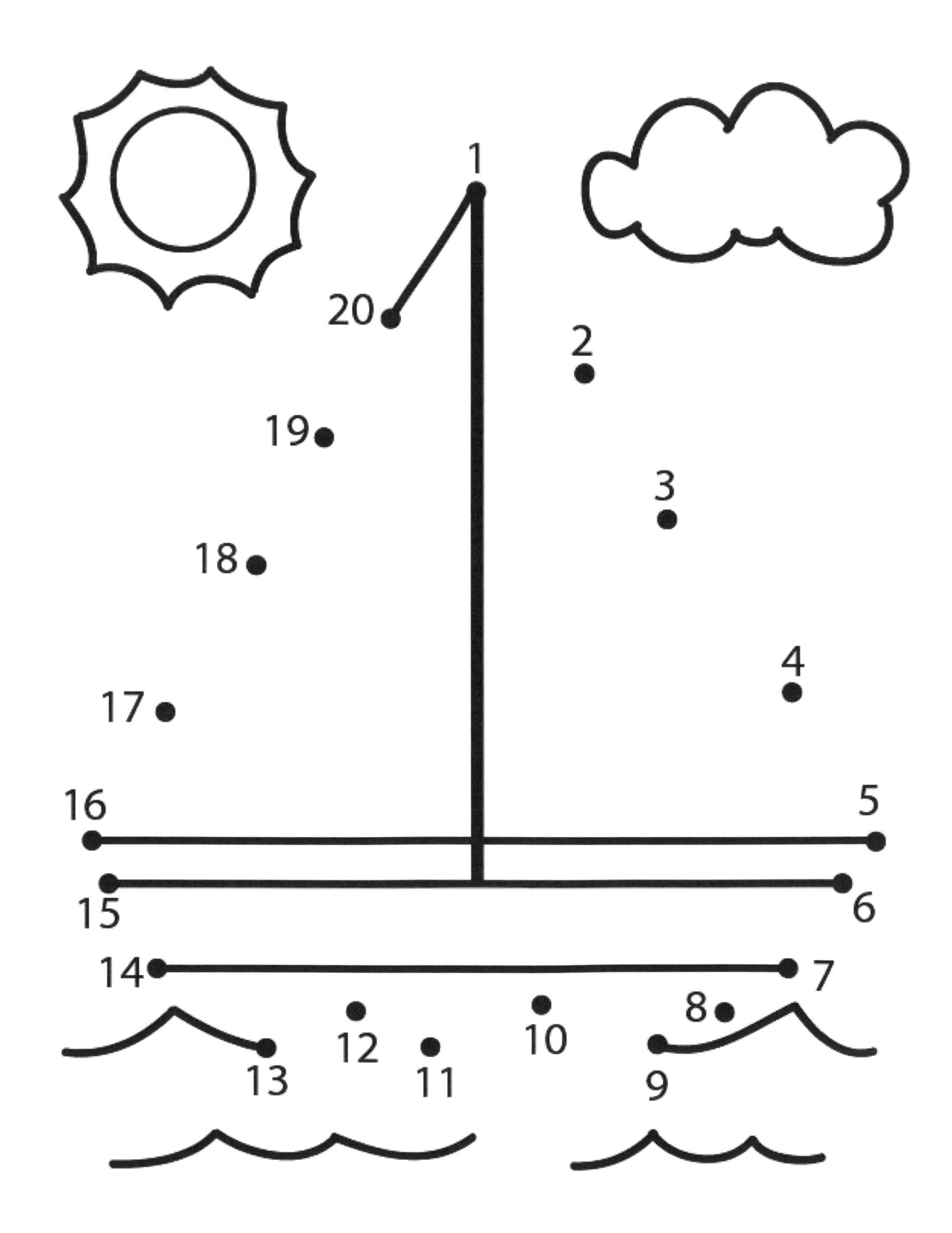

cut along line

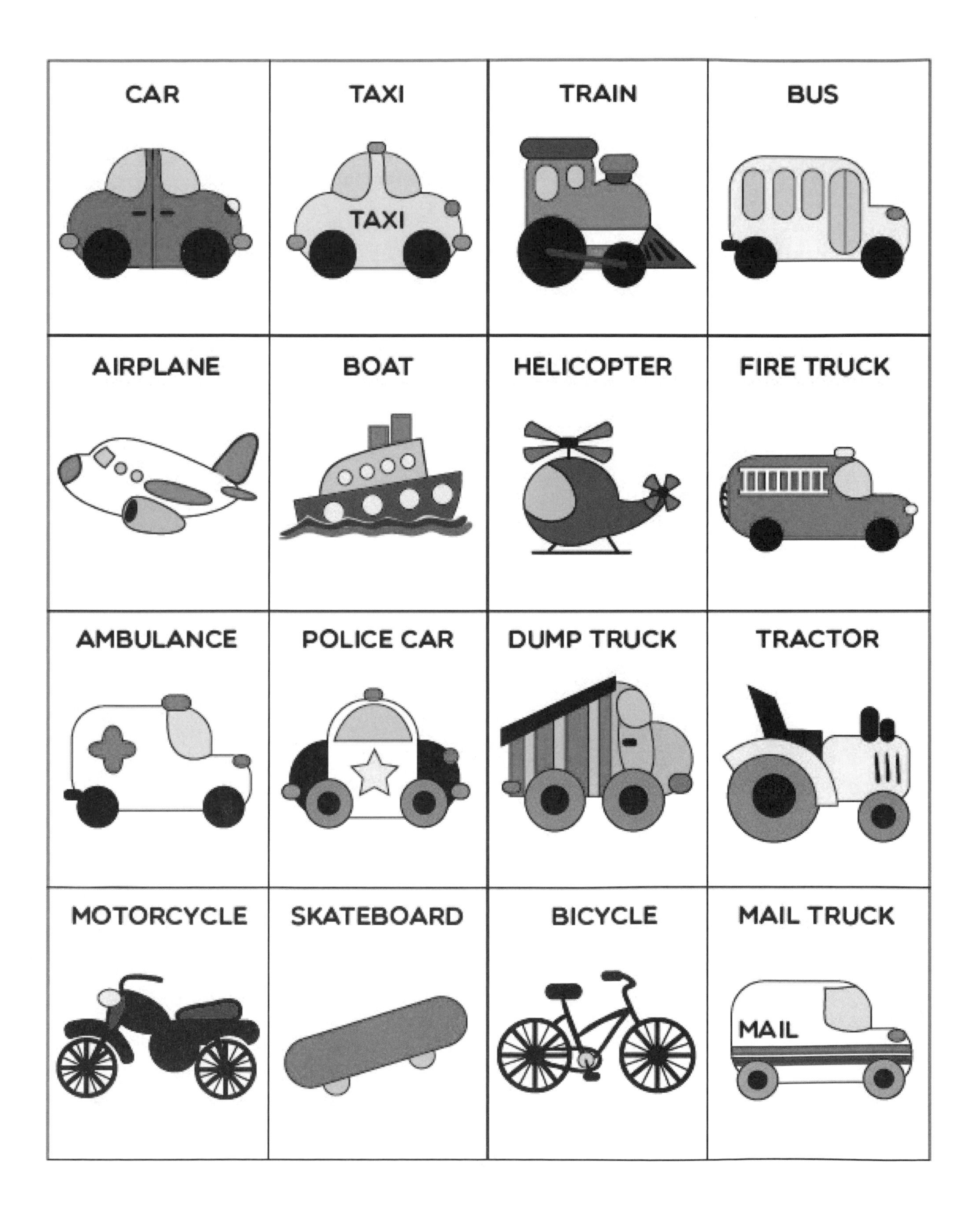

cut along line

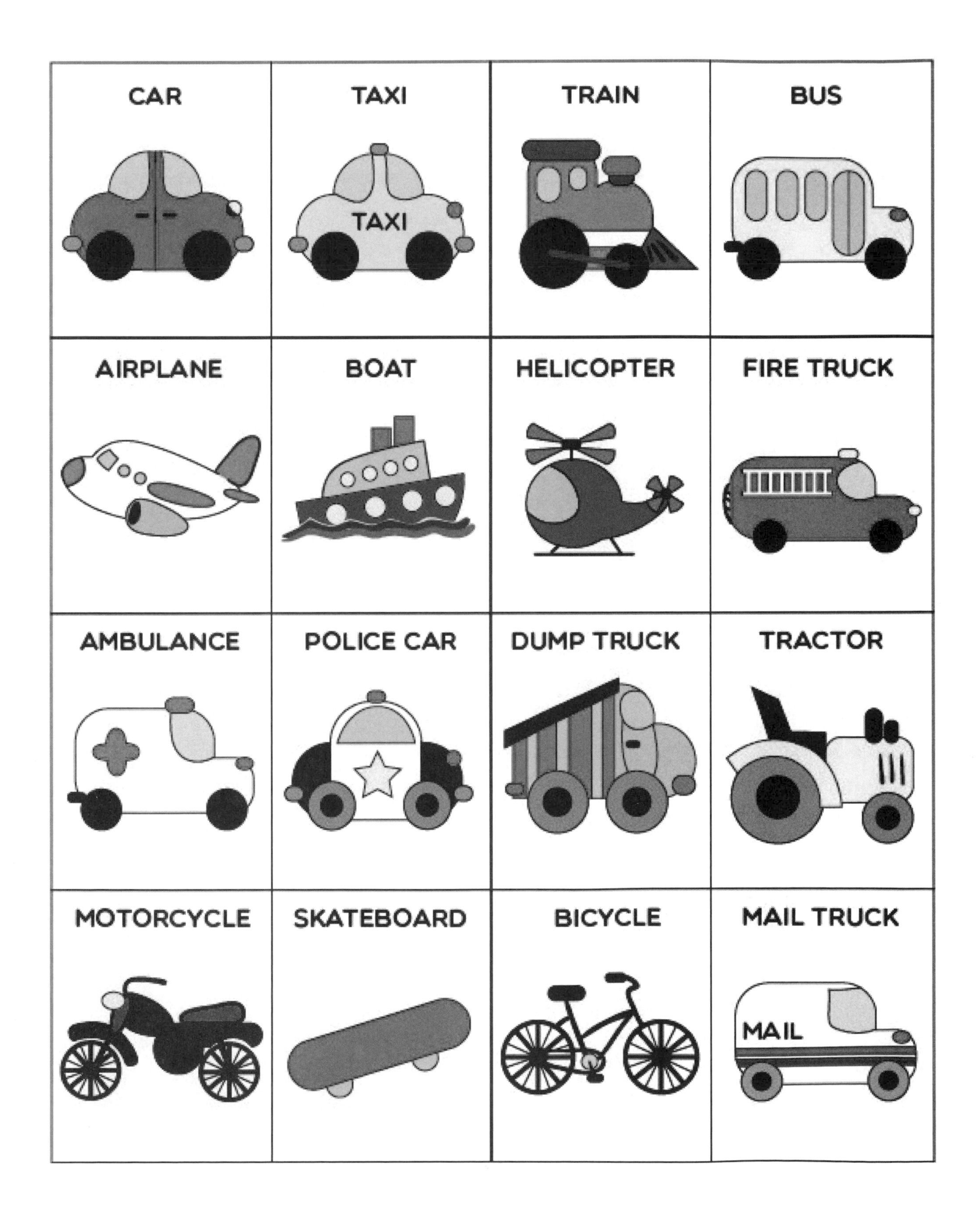

cut along line

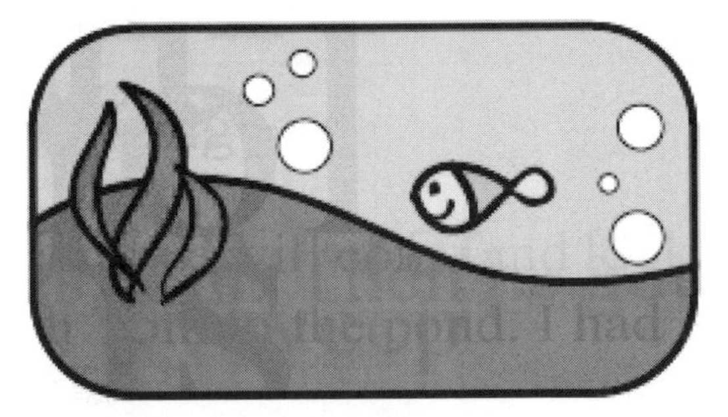

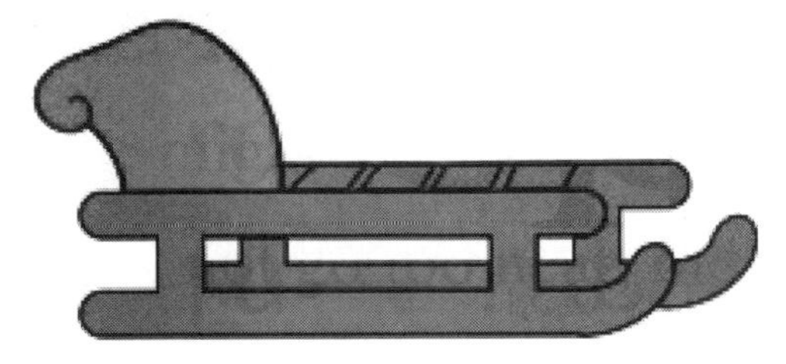

cut along line

WHICH ONE IS DIFFERENT?

cut along line

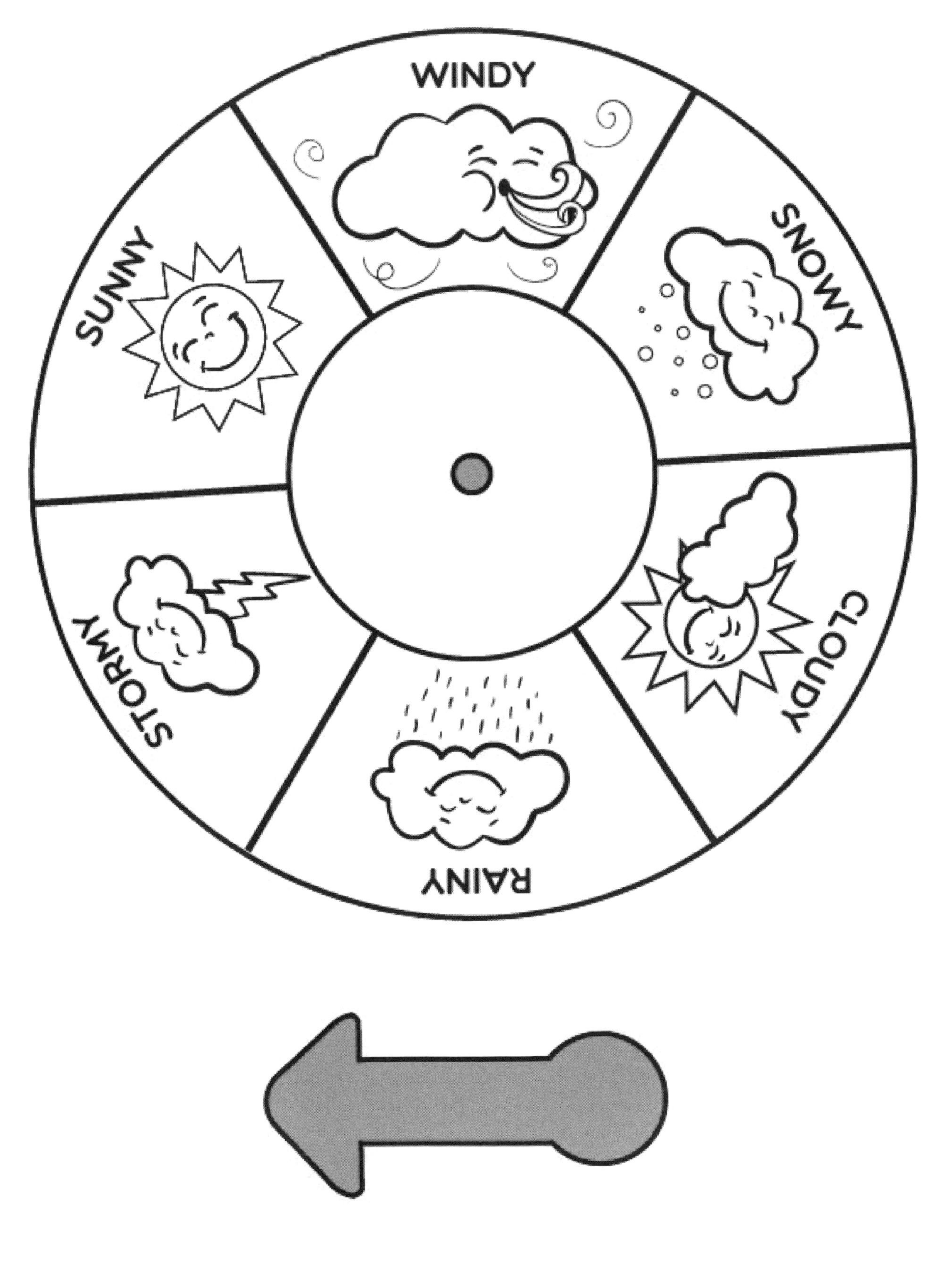

cut along line

cut along line

cut along line

cut along line

Thank you for welcoming me into your home!
I hope you and your child liked learning together with this book!

If you enjoyed this book, it would mean so much to me
if you wrote a review so other moms can learn from your experience.

Autumn@BestMomIdeas.com

Discover Autumn's Other Books

Early Learning Series

Early Learning Workbook Series